Business Agreements

Made Easy™

About the author

Yvette Hoskings-James worked as an in-house lawyer for various multinational organisations before setting up a business consultancy. Her business consultancy provides advice and training/workshops on risk management, contracts and business law matters. Yvette is also a voluntary business mentor through a nationwide voluntary mentor scheme.

Business Agreements Made Easy
by Yvette Hoskings-James

© 2005 Lawpack Publishing Limited

The right of Yvette Hoskings-James to be identified as the author of this work has been asserted by her in accordance with the Copyright, Designs and Patents Act 1988.

Lawpack Publishing Limited
76–89 Alscot Road
London SE1 3AW

www.lawpack.co.uk

All rights reserved
Printed in Great Britain

ISBN 1 904053 84 X

Exclusion of Liability and Disclaimer

Table of contents

Introduction

The focus of this book is business-to-business contracts for the sale of goods or the supply of services to clients. This book is a general guide to some of the main commercial and legal issues, as well as the pitfalls which can arise in relation to these business agreements.

Contracts should not dominate the relationship with a client or supplier as they are only part of the 'overall picture' – albeit an essential part. Contracts are looked at in a practical and commercial context, not just a legal perspective. Various commercial and legal issues which occur throughout the contract process (e.g. from pre-contract to the end of the contract) are looked at.

In this book most of the issues are looked at from your perspective when dealing with your clients. They are also relevant when dealing with your suppliers or subcontractors.

The book is not intended to deal with any specific industry. It is intended to cover general simple business agreements for the supply of goods and/or services. For example, it does not cover agency agreements or distribution agreements, employment contracts, contracts for sale of businesses or research and development agreements.

This book is not intended to be a substitute for legal or other professional advice or an exhaustive examination of all the commercial and legal issues which can arise. If you require legal advice or other guidance, you should contact a lawyer or suitable professional adviser.

You may have specific needs and requirements. Therefore, it cannot be guaranteed that any example documents in this book are suitable for any purposes for which you may use them. No responsibility can be accepted for any use of any document or information in this book (including any action you decide not to take).

While care has been taken in producing this book, the correctness or accuracy of any of the content is not guaranteed. This is because laws change and courts make decisions which affect the interpretation and understanding of the law.

Any references to laws and regulations in this book are to English and Welsh law and regulations, and they are subject to change.

Yvette Hoskings-James
April 2005

CHAPTER 1

Prevention is better than cure

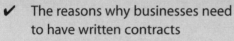

What you'll find in this chapter

✔ The reasons why businesses need to have written contracts

✔ The problem with verbal agreements

The reasons why businesses need to have written contracts

Many people think contracts are complex and written in some obscure ancient language. Written contracts are sometimes viewed as a hindrance when business people are in a rush to do a deal, but they are an important part of any business transaction and they can be written in plain English! They also form an essential part of effective risk management. In this chapter we are going to look at the importance of having written contracts.

First, it is important to understand the meaning of the term 'contract'.

'I don't have a contract – I didn't sign anything!'

The above is a common misunderstanding – the law recognises verbal or written contracts. They can also be made over the internet or by email. For example, many people now use the internet to buy CDs and books, as well as their weekly food shopping. There are only a few contracts which are required by English and Welsh law to be in writing (one important example is a guarantee, which we will look at later in this chapter).

A contract is a legally binding agreement which creates various enforceable rights and obligations. For example, you enter into a contract with your client to sell him a laptop for £1,000. You deliver the laptop to his premises. You have a right to be paid £1,000 and your client has an obligation to pay you £1,000. If your client refuses to pay you, you can enforce your right to receive payment by taking legal action.

Certain requirements need to be complied with to create a valid and enforceable contract; these requirements will be looked at in further detail in chapter 3.

If you look at your daily activities, you will realise that contracts (usually verbal) are made throughout the day. You buy goods and services every day as a consumer (i.e. as a person who is not acting in the course of his business). For example, when you go out at lunchtime to buy a sandwich or a CD and when you go to the hairdresser/barber for a haircut or when you buy a new suit.

Business contracts can also be verbal contracts. For example, a client may ring you and ask you to perform a particular service. You agree and start performing the service the next day. It is not ideal to conduct business on the basis of verbal contracts. This is because business contracts can often involve large amounts of money. There are usually various details and terms which need to be properly agreed. It can be difficult to prove the terms which have been agreed without a written record. Also, business-to-business contracts are subject to less protection than business-to-consumer contracts. Consumers have certain rights which automatically apply in relation to consumer contracts. Details of these matters can be found on the Department of Trade and Industry's (DTI) website at www.dti.gov.uk/ccp.

 As business-to-business contracts are not subject to the same restrictions as business-to-consumer contracts, businesses are generally free to negotiate the terms of their contracts with other businesses. So, if you make a bad deal, you will usually be stuck with it.

'I am too busy to sort out formal paperwork ...'

You are busy running your business and you want to get the deal done, so you agree to proceed on the basis of a verbal agreement ...

Many problems are often caused by entering into verbal agreements. These problems are frustrating, take up a lot of management time and cost you a lot of money.

The problem with verbal agreements

One of the main problems with verbal agreements or informal understandings, such as a 'gentleman's agreement', is that your client or supplier may have a completely different view of the agreement. You may think you have a good relationship with your client or supplier – if you have a dispute with him, you will soon find out if he has the same view of the relationship.

Things that can go wrong with verbal agreements include:

- **Fading memories:** details that have been verbally agreed can easily be forgotten (intentionally or unintentionally) as time passes.

- **Contract terms:** there is no written record of the matters agreed, such as key terms (e.g. a detailed description of services or deliverables, price, payment and schedule).

- **Payment:** if there is a disagreement, it may be difficult to be paid for all the work you have carried out if the price and payment terms are not clearly recorded in a written contract.

- **Changes:** if you do not have a clear record of your scope of services/work or deliverables, it can be difficult to get paid for any matters which you regard as changes/variations to your scope of services/work or deliverables. Often, this is because the client will regard his requests for further work as being part of the existing contract, while you regard it as additional work. The result is that either you end up in dispute or you carry out the additional work for no payment.

- **Liabilities:** if you do not agree a limit to your liability, in the event of a dispute which ends up going to court, the courts will use the law to work out your liability. If you are the unsuccessful person who has to pay compensation, you may have to pay much more than you think you should pay. Further information regarding liabilities, including examples of limitation of liability clauses, are included in chapter 4.

- **Misunderstanding:** lack of clear agreement regarding contract requirements and obligations increases the risk of misunderstanding and performance problems.

'What about starting work while the contract terms are being negotiated?'

Your client may be in a rush to start work before a formal written contract is agreed and entered into. A common practice in this situation is for the client to issue a letter advising you of his intention to award you the contract and authorising you to start work while the contract negotiations are taking place. These letters are known as 'letters of intent'. They also describe some of the key terms of the deal (if these have been agreed), such as the price and scope of work.

The problem with letters of intent is that sometimes they can be legally binding and sometimes not. The legal status of a letter of intent depends on the specific facts in relation to the use of the letter and the language used in it. Unfortunately, when people enter into a letter of intent they are not always clear as to whether they intend the letter to be legally binding. The letters are often vaguely drafted. People often end up using letters of intent and never entering into a formal written contract with many matters remaining to be agreed. This can lead to a problem when there are disputes, such as a disagreement about payment or quality of work.

 Letters of intent should not be used as a substitute for a contract. It is recommended that you obtain professional advice if you have to work on the basis of a letter of intent.

'My client has not paid, so I talked to his client. He told me not to worry and to keep on working because he has given me his word that he will sort out any money I should be paid'

As already mentioned, contracts are not required to be in writing, apart from in a few exceptions (these exceptions will be discussed in this book where relevant). One important exception relates to guarantees. Business guarantees are usually used to provide security for the payment or performance of the contract's obligations. For example, you may have to give your bank a personal guarantee in relation to a loan that it gives to your company which you have just set up. Companies have a separate legal identity from their owners and directors. The bank may be concerned that the company may not be able to comply with its payment obligations in relation to the loan. It will want to be certain that it can recover its money. Therefore, it will require some form of security for the loan, i.e. a guarantee from you (assuming you have assets such as a house or savings). This guarantee makes you personally responsible for repaying the loan, in the event that the company does not comply with its payment obligations.

If you are supplying goods or services to your client, you will obviously want to get paid. You should never rely on the 'word' of a third party (i.e. someone other than your client) if he agrees to make payment of the money owed to you by your client or the takeover of your client's payment obligations to you in the event of his failure to pay you.

 Such promises constitute a guarantee and can only be enforced if they are in writing and signed by the person making the promises (or someone authorised on his behalf).

For example, Mr X is the director of several companies including Companies A and B. You may have a contract with his new company, Company A, which has just been set up. As it is a new company, it has no money, but you are told verbally not to worry as all payments will be made through Company B, which has been trading for several years and has plenty of money. Companies A and B have two separate legal identities. You should not accept this arrangement. In order to make sure Company

B pays you, you should get a written guarantee from Company B, signed by Company B.

The Actionstrength real case described below went to court and demonstrates the problems of relying on a promise of payment from someone who is not your client.

Case study: Actionstrength Limited v International Glass Engineering and others (2003)

A company called Actionstrength entered into a contract with another business ('construction company') for the supply of construction workers.

The construction company needed these workers to fulfil a contract with a third company, called St-Gobain, to build a factory.

Some months into the project the construction company owed Actionstrength several thousands of pounds. On experiencing problems getting paid, Actionstrength went directly to St-Gobain, and informed St-Gobain that without receipt of payment, it would withdraw the construction workers from the project.

Actionstrength continued to supply workers on the understanding that St-Gobain had agreed to make sure that payments would be received and, if necessary, instead of paying the construction company, St-Gobain would make direct payments to Actionstrength.

Actionstrength continued supplying construction workers until it was eventually owed £1.3 million.

It sued both the construction company and St-Gobain (on the basis of the verbal agreement). Unfortunately, the construction company went into liquidation; therefore, Actionstrength was unable to recover any money from it.

The court decided that the plaintiff was also unable to recover any money from St- Gobain. This was because the verbal promises/ agreement of St-Gobain constituted a guarantee of the debt owed by the construction company to Actionstrength, in which case, such a guarantee could only be valid and enforceable if it had been in writing and signed by St-Gobain (or someone authorised to sign on its behalf). The decision of the court was based on legislation which is over 300 years old (called the Statute of Frauds 1677).

This sad tale demonstrates the disastrous consequences of relying on verbal agreements.

'OK. Can you describe some of the key benefits of a written contract?'

Written contracts should not be seen as a necessary evil. They are part of a professional approach to business. Written contracts help define the parameters of the commercial relationship between you and your client or supplier. They provide an opportunity to set out the details of the deal you have agreed rather than you relying on assumptions. The main benefits include:

- **Clear contract terms:** agreed and recorded in writing including key terms, such as:
  - Scope of work/services or project deliverables
  - Time schedule
  - Standard and quality of work/services or project deliverables
  - Liabilities
  - Price and payment terms.
- **Limits of liability:** you can include a limit on your liability in the contract.
- **Clarity:** clarity regarding rights and obligations of you and your client or supplier. In the event of a dispute, a written contract provides evidence of the matters agreed and can assist in resolving disputes and getting paid.
- **Improved risk management:**
  - Insurers look at a variety of factors when assessing risk and setting your insurance premiums. They often require details regarding your risk management procedures and the type of contracts you enter into (including copies of your standard terms and conditions).
  - Directors have responsibility for managing their companies. They have overall responsibility for risk management practices

and procedures. Well-drafted written contracts/standard terms and conditions will assist them in managing the risks in the business. The ability to demonstrate good risk management practices and procedures can also assist you when you are trying to raise finance for your business (e.g. from lenders and potential investors).

'I know verbal agreements are not ideal, so what can I do?'

 You should have your own standard terms and conditions which you use or a properly negotiated contract. However, as we all know, we are not living in Utopia and this does not always happen.

If work has to start without a formal written contract, you should, as a minimum, record the key terms and matters agreed and confirm your understanding to your client or supplier in writing. You should also ask your client or supplier to acknowledge the receipt of your letter and confirm his written agreement. This is not ideal, as not all matters will have been dealt with; a properly negotiated contract or your standard terms and conditions are the best policy. But it is better than nothing. In the event of a dispute, it will assist you in proving the matters you have agreed.

Summary of key points

- Verbal contracts or informal agreements often lead to disputes or debts being written off because of misunderstandings or a lack of proof regarding the matters agreed.

- Written contracts set out the mutual understanding, obligations and rights of you and your client or supplier.

- A properly drafted, written contract will provide a record of the terms agreed; this will assist in minimising disputes.

- If no formal contract is entered into, record the key terms in writing and get your client or supplier to confirm his written agreement.

- Guarantees: always ensure that any agreement with a third party to pay money owed to you by your client is in writing and is signed by the person or by the authorised representative of the company giving the guarantee. You should obtain proof from the company that the person signing upon behalf of the company has the authority to sign the guarantee. As guarantees are not routine agreements, the guarantee will usually need to be authorised by the board of directors and they will authorise a specific director (such as the Managing Director) to sign the guarantee.

- Letters of intent should not be used as a substitute for a written contract.

CHAPTER 2

Planning and forethought

What you'll find in this chapter

✔ Matters that you need to consider before you enter into a contract

Matters that you need to consider before you enter into a contract

Have you carried out work for a client and lived to regret it? Was the work more hassle than it was worth because your client had unreasonable expectations, you underpriced the job, your client did not pay on time or you had to work to a tight deadline? There can be many reasons for projects or work not going well. Sometimes unexpected events can occur. Sometimes the problems are due to poor planning before you made the deal with the client.

To help avoid some of these problems, you can ask yourself some of the following questions before you make the deal.

'Can I do the job?'

This may seem obvious, but it is an important question. Do you or your employees have the skills or experience to do the work? If you don't and things go wrong, you could find yourself on the end of a legal claim.

'Do I want to do the job?'

You may decide that you do not want the job. Have a look at your resources. If you and your staff are working to full capacity, you may decide that you are currently too busy to take on any additional work. If you are overstretched, there is a risk that you may not carry out work to the required standard.

'Is the price right?'

If you supply goods or products, it should be fairly straightforward to work out how much you will sell them for. For example, you will be able to work out a price based on the cost of the goods/products, your overheads and profit margin.

If you provide services, you should look at the time and effort you will need to put into providing your service. You then need to make an assessment about the amount of money you should be paid. You may decide to charge an hourly fee or a fixed price. If you work on a fixed-price basis, you need to have a very clear description of the work or services agreed with your client. Your client needs to have a clear understanding of what he will be getting for his fixed price and so do you!

 If you underprice your work, you could end up feeling overworked and resentful.

'How will I get paid?'

There are some practical things you can do, such as carrying out credit checks and asking for advance payments.

Managing cash flow is a major issue for all businesses (small or large). Look at your cash flow. If you are using suppliers who need advance payment, you need to ensure that you obtain advance payment from your client. Otherwise, you will be stuck in the middle where you have paid your suppliers in full and are chasing your client for payment.

> **TIP** You may want to consider a payment schedule linked to the progress of the work or services you supply.

You should carry out some financial checks if you have concerns about your client's ability to pay you. However, if you do have major concerns about this, perhaps you should not be carrying out work for him. Nothing is more frustrating than carrying out work and not being paid because someone has disappeared or wound up his business.

There are a number of places where you can obtain information about the financial condition of a person or his business. A few useful websites are shown below:

- You can carry out a bankruptcy search against individuals at the Insolvency Service's website: www.insolvency.gov.uk/guidanceleaflets/register.htm.

- Information is available about companies and limited liability partnerships at the Companies House's website at www.companies house.gov.uk/info. Various types of information and reports are available. Some basic information is free, while you have to pay for other certain information.

- Details of County court judgments can be found at the Registry Trust's website at www.registry-trust.org.uk.

- Alternatively, you may prefer to obtain a report from a credit reference agency. Details of credit reference agencies can be found on the Registry Trust's website.

'Can I keep my promises?'

Sometimes people make exaggerated or misleading claims or statements about their products or services. These claims can be included in their advertisements, proposals or in statements they make verbally to clients when they are negotiating or trying to win a project or work. Sometimes these claims or statements can end up being incorporated as contract terms in the contract with the client. Alternatively, a client may rely on the statements and decide to enter into a contract. The supplier may then find himself having to deal with a legal action due to these false or misleading statements.

You should be careful to make sure that this does not happen to you. A well-written contract can provide some assistance by confirming that all the terms of the deal are included in the written contract. However, this will not give you absolute protection as these clauses (which attempt to exclude pre-contract representations) need to comply with a reasonableness test (discussed in chapter 4). Also, you cannot exclude liability for fraudulent misrepresentations. The simple solution is not to make statements which are false or misleading.

'Who owns the intellectual property rights?'

Intellectual rights protect creative and inventive outputs and work. For example, a patent can protect your invention, while copyright can protect a book that you have written and your company logo may be protected by a registered trade mark. Intellectual property rights can be valuable assets to a business.

Depending on the nature of your business, you may want to own the relevant intellectual property rights in relation to your products and perhaps give your client a licence (i.e. permission) to use them. Alternatively, your client may want to own the relevant intellectual property rights. To avoid any misunderstanding, ownership should be dealt with in a written contract. Intellectual property rights can be dealt with in various ways, such as by licensing or assignment (i.e. transfer). Assignments should be in writing and signed.

 A detailed discussion about intellectual property rights is outside the scope of this book. Appropriate professional advice should be obtained in relation to intellectual property rights.

'Will I need to use suppliers or subcontractors?'

You may need to use suppliers or subcontractors to assist you in supplying your products or services. A subcontracting relationship occurs when you pass on your responsibilities to another business (i.e. a subcontractor) for carrying out your work or part of your work (i.e. you enter into a subcontract). For example, you enter into a contract with a client to manufacture an engine. You buy all the materials and equipment required from your usual suppliers. You decide not to assemble and manufacture the engine and enter into a contract (i.e. a subcontract) with another company to carry out the assembly and manufacturing of the engine. As you are responsible to your client, it is important to manage effectively the risks in relation to your suppliers or subcontractors.

- **Key requirements**

    If your client has certain essential requirements, you need to ensure that these are reflected in your written contract with your supplier or subcontractor; for example, detailed scope of work, time schedule, quality of product/work.

- **Copyright**

    Ownership of copyright and other intellectual property rights may need to be considered. For example, the general rule in relation to copyright is that it belongs to the creator unless otherwise agreed. This rule does not apply to employees. Employers own copyright to work created by their employees in the course of their employment.

    If you have a supplier carrying out work for you, you may want an assignment (i.e. transfer) of these rights (which should be in writing and signed). If this is the case, you should include this requirement in your written contract.

    The Dr. Martens case below provides a useful illustration of some of the problems which can arise in relation to copyright.

Case study: R Griggs Limited and others v Evans and others (2005)

Dr. Martens footwear is well known throughout the world. The owner and manufacturer of these famous boots and shoes ('Griggs') decided in 1988 to combine two trade marks that it used into one combined logo. It asked its advertising agency to carry out the work. The agency then paid a freelancer to carry out the work. No written contract was entered into between any of the parties. No discussion took place regarding the ownership of copyright.

In 2002, the freelancer assigned (i.e. transferred) the copyright in the combined logo to an Australian competitor. Naturally, this matter ended up going to court. The court confirmed that while the freelancer may have been the legal owner of the copyright in the logo, Griggs had more than just an implied licence or permission to use the logo. It had a right to stop other people from using the logo and to have all legal rights to the copyright assigned to it by court order.

This summary of the case is not a comprehensive statement about the laws of copyright. However, it does demonstrate how important it is to deal with the ownership of copyright in your contract with your supplier before he starts working for you.

- **Ownership**

  Ownership of products/goods (if applicable) supplied by your supplier should be considered. Most suppliers will want full payment before the ownership of their goods is passed to you. This may impact your cash flow, as discussed above.

- **Insurance**

  In the event of any problems with the supplier's or subcontractor's work, the work may need to be reperformed or legal action may need to be taken against the supplier or subcontractor. You want to make sure that he has enough money to be able to reperform work or pay for any losses or damages. You may want to ask your suppliers or subcontractors to carry insurance and provide you with proof of their insurance (e.g. their current certificate of insurance). If you use them regularly, ask them to provide a certificate on an annual basis.

Summary of key points

- Don't do the work if you know that you don't have the necessary skills to carry out the work properly.
- Make sure you charge the right price for the work (i.e. do not undercharge).
- Look at your cash flow and include payment terms which reflect your cash flow requirements.

- Carry out financial checks if you think they are necessary.

- Do not make misleading or false claims.

- Deal with ownership of intellectual property rights.

- Use written contracts with your suppliers/subcontractors which reflect your client's requirements.

- Ask your suppliers/subcontractors for insurance certificates.

CHAPTER 3

Negotiating contracts

What you'll find in this chapter
✔ The ideal situation
✔ 'Why do I need to understand the requirements for contract formation?'
✔ The basic requirements for contract formation
✔ Contract terms
✔ Practical tips to avoid disputes
✔ Dealing with other businesses' standard terms and conditions
✔ Battle of the forms
✔ Practical tips on standard business terms

The ideal situation for any business is for it to be able to supply its products or services in accordance with its standard terms and conditions. You may not be in that position and will have to negotiate your contracts with your clients. You may also find yourself in the situation where you have to negotiate changes to your standard terms. It is important that you are able to recognise the common problems so that you can avoid them. This chapter looks at these problems and some of the steps you can take to avoid them.

The ideal situation

During the negotiation stage, you will try to agree the terms of the deal.

This can be quite a straightforward or lengthy process depending on the nature of your business and the requirements of the person whom you are negotiating with. It can take place through meetings, telephone conversations, emails and letters. After this process is completed, all the terms of the deal should be agreed. You should ideally record all the agreed terms in a written contract which is signed by both parties. The usual process is to sign and date two copies of the contract, so each party has a copy signed by both parties. Signatures are not usually required to make a contract legally binding (except for certain agreements such as guarantees and assignments of copyright as discussed in the previous chapters). However, they provide a useful method of confirming that the persons who have entered into the contract have agreed to the contract terms.

As we do not live in an ideal world, a number of problems can occur, which will be looked at in this chapter. One of the first issues which needs to be looked at is the basic requirements needed for a binding and enforceable contract.

As previously mentioned in chapter 1, a contract is a legally binding agreement which creates various enforceable rights and obligations. Certain requirements are needed in order for a contract to be properly formed so that it is valid and enforceable. Sometimes problems can occur when these key requirements are overlooked at the contract negotiation stage.

'Why do I need to understand the requirements for contract formation?'

You may be wondering why it is important to understand the legal technicalities for contract formation. It is important to understand these requirements because of the practical and commercial impact that mistakes in contract formation can have on your business.

Many disputes often go to court because one person is asserting that there was a contract and that he wants payment for his work, while the person defending the claim will assert that there wasn't a contract. Alternatively, situations can arise where both parties accept that there is a contractual arrangement in place, but they do not agree on the terms. The job of the court is to reach an objective decision. This will usually involve it deciding whether a valid contract has been formed and making a determination as to the terms of the contract. This is not usually a straightforward process and will involve the court making a decision based on the facts and evidence which are presented to it.

The basic requirements for contract formation

The basic requirements for the formation of a contract are the offer, acceptance, consideration and intention to create legal relations.

The offer

You can think of an offer as a clear promise or statement that proposes to do something (which is usually subject to certain conditions) and that is intended to be a binding commitment as soon as it is accepted. For example, you may give a quote for some work (which contains details of the price and payment terms, detailed description of the work, etc.) subject to your standard terms and conditions (see page 24 for further information regarding making your quote subject to your standard terms and conditions).

The acceptance

The acceptance is a clear acceptance of what has been proposed (i.e. the offer) without any qualifications. If we continue to use the above example, the client accepts your quote and signs your standard terms and conditions and returns them to you. He has accepted the offer and you and the client are now agreed.

The acceptance must match the terms of the offer. In other words, there should be no variations made to the offer by the person who has accepted the offer. Insignificant variations can be disregarded. The terms of the agreement must be clear. In relation to this example, if the client had responded stating that he would accept your quotation on the basis that the price is reduced by ten per cent, this would not be an acceptance of your offer. This is really a counter-offer. You then need to decide if you reject this counter-offer, accept it or make an alternative offer.

The problem of whether an offer or a counter-offer has been accepted often arises in relation to disputes based on verbal agreements or agreements where all the terms have not been clearly agreed. It is when the dispute takes place that the client and supplier realise that they have different ideas about what was offered and what was accepted.

The consideration

Consideration can be thought of as an exchange of something of value (even if it is of minimal value) for a promise; usually, the payment of money in exchange for the supply of services or goods. If we look at the example of a seller who enters into a contract to sell a computer to a buyer, the payment of money by the buyer is consideration for the promise of the seller to deliver the computer. Delivery of the computer by the seller is consideration for the promise by the buyer to pay the seller. Accordingly, consideration is required for a contract to be enforceable, while informal promises are not legally enforceable as there is no consideration.

The intention to create legal relations

This intention is usually assumed to exist in relation to transactions carried out in the course of business.

Contract terms

The terms of a contract must be clear. If they are not clear, it may not be possible to enforce them. Contract terms will be discussed in further detail in chapter 4.

Case study: Twintec Limited v GSE Building & Civil Engineering Limited (2003)

The Twintec case is a typical example of a situation that arises in many businesses. It provides a useful illustration of the basic requirements for contract formation. It also demonstrates the problems with documents which are regarded as letters of intent (see chapter 1 for more information). In addition, it demonstrates that contracts do not have to consist in one formal document. The terms of a contract can be contained in several documents, as well as through verbal agreements. However, this situation can present difficulties in proving all the agreed terms.

Twintec specialises in the design and construction of industrial flooring. Twintec claimed to have a contract with GSE Building & Civil Engineering Limited ('GSE') to carry out some work. Twintec carried out some initial work (i.e. design work and ordering materials) in the belief that it had a contract with GSE. After Twintec had carried out the work, it found out that GSE had appointed another company to carry out the work. GSE argued that no legally binding contract was entered into. The matter went to court and it was decided that there was a legally binding contract. Therefore, GSE was liable to pay for the work. The decision was based on the evidence of witnesses and documents which included:

- a written quotation from Twintec;

- evidence of a meeting between representatives of Twintec and GSE to discuss and agree certain matters in relation to the project; and

- a letter from Twintec to GSE confirming GSE's intent to award the order for the work to Twintec (the letter of intent).

The key points from this case are as follows:

1. The quotation constituted an offer.

2. The fact that a document is called a letter of intent does not have any legal significance. In the event of a dispute, the courts will look at each case on its facts. In this case, it was clear that GSE wanted to use Twintec's services quickly and the letter of intent was to be regarded as a commitment by GSE to use Twintec. On the basis of the facts of this case, the letter of intent was an acceptance by GSE of Twintec's offer.

3. No detailed analysis took place regarding consideration. Here, the court simply confirmed that there was no issue regarding consideration, i.e. this requirement was satisfied. Consideration was discussed earlier in this chapter (e.g. the supply of services in return for a promise of payment).

4. The court noted from the evidence given that it was clear at the meeting between the representatives of Twintec and GSE that they intended to do a deal. The court concluded that Twintec and GSE had the intention to create legal relations between the two companies.

5. The court objectively concluded that the basic requirements for a valid contract existed.

The judge rejected the evidence of some of the witnesses, as she did not believe their evidence in relation to certain matters, demonstrating the problems on having to rely on the evidence of witnesses to prove the existence of a contract, rather than using a written contract containing all the relevant terms.

Practical tips to avoid disputes

To avoid ending up in disputes, there are some practical steps you can take:

*   If you want your quotation or proposal to be an offer which can be accepted by your client, you need to make it clear that it is subject to your standard terms and conditions; for example, 'Our proposal is subject to our attached standard terms and conditions. These terms and conditions shall apply to any contract we enter into with you for the supply of the goods described in our proposal'. Your proposal or quotation should clearly state the details of your offer and requirements; for example, a detailed description of the services or products to be supplied, the price, payment terms (including whether VAT is payable), delivery arrangements and any specific requirements you have.

*   You should include your standard terms and conditions with your quotation or proposal together with an acceptance form for signature by your client. The form should make it clear that acceptance of the quotation or proposal includes an acceptance of the terms and conditions; for example, 'We [*insert name of client*] accept your proposal dated [*insert date*] and your standard terms and conditions

for the supply of the goods described in your proposal'. You can also state that the terms must be signed and returned to you. If you do not intend your quotation or proposal to be an offer which can be accepted, you should make that clear, otherwise you may end up entering into a contract on terms that you do not want. See comments later in this chapter regarding making quotations or proposals 'subject to contract'.

- If your client responds with changes to your quotation or proposal (which may take place in discussions over the telephone or meetings, as well as written responses), issue a revised quotation or proposal subject to your standard terms and conditions (i.e. including your standard terms and acceptance form) recording all the changes which you have agreed. Remember, a response to your offer which includes changes or qualifications is not an acceptance. It is counter-offer – therefore you can choose to accept it, reject it or make another offer.

- If negotiations have taken place over a period of time (e.g. via correspondence, telephone calls and meetings), it is important to ensure that all the terms are properly recorded before you start work. You should confirm the specific matters agreed in writing and include them in your contract.

- If you do not use standard terms and conditions for your business, you need to negotiate a contract. You should make it clear that the quotation or proposal is not an offer. For example, you should state that any quotation or proposal you send is 'subject to contract' or 'subject to negotiating mutually acceptable contract terms and conditions'. This will indicate that there is no intention to enter into a legally binding agreement until the terms have been agreed. Using these expressions will not provide you with protection against any claim that a legally-binding contract has been formed or prevent a contract being formed if you behave in a manner which is inconsistent with these statements. For example, a contract may come into existence if work starts on the basis of a letter of intent. Your essential terms or requirements should be included in the quotation or proposal. This will ensure that you do not forget to include them during the negotiations and in the finalised contract; for example, a detailed description of services, price, payment terms, delivery arrangements and any specific requirements you may have.

- It is also a good idea to put a time limit on the acceptance of a quotation or proposal (often known as a 'validity period'). In the event that you have sent out a proposal or quotation in the form of an offer and your client does not reply within a short space of time, you may think that he is not interested. In the meantime, you may have decided to increase your prices. Your client may now decide to accept your offer and you will be stuck with carrying out the work at the old prices because you did not state that the prices and other parts of your proposal were only valid for a limited period (e.g. 60 days).

- Avoid working on the basis of a letter of intent. As discussed in chapter 1 and in the Twintec case, letters of intent do not have any specific legal status. They can be legally binding or not legally binding, depending on the specific facts, including the language of the document. If you have to work on the basis of a letter of intent, you should consider obtaining professional advice to ensure that it is drafted to protect your position. For example, if you are carrying out work for a client, you will want a legally binding commitment that your client will make payment for the work carried out under the letter of the intent.

Dealing with other businesses' standard terms and conditions

If you work under the standard terms of other businesses (e.g. your clients' or suppliers'/subcontractors' terms), you should read them carefully. If you do not understand any of the terms, obtain professional advice. If things go wrong, claiming you did not understand the terms you signed will not help you. Business people are expected to take steps to manage risks in their business. It is not the job of the court to rectify a bad deal.

Standard terms of business of your client or supplier/subcontractor will usually be drafted to provide them with maximum benefit and protection. The checklist in Appendix 1 will provide you with a list of some of the points that you need to be aware of.

Battle of the forms

'Battle of the forms' is an expression lawyers often use to describe negotiations between businesses based on the exchange of the standard terms and conditions of each business.

A typical battle may take place as follows:

You may offer to carry out work for your client on your standard terms of business and send him a copy. Your client replies confirming that he wants you to carry out the work, but on his standard terms of business. He sends you a copy of his standard terms; for example, this might be in the form of the client's standard purchase order with his terms printed on the back.

This is the battle of the forms. You can either accept his terms or inform him that you do not accept them and that your terms apply, or you may negotiate a contract that is acceptable to both of you.

If you just start working without responding to the client, you may find yourself in the position of having accepted the client's terms – this is the usual position. However, depending on the circumstances, it is possible that neither sets of terms apply and if the matter went to court, the court may decide that the terms implied by law apply! Implied terms can be in relation to the quality of the goods, the standard of services, the time for payment, the rights of termination and other matters. These implied terms may not be as favourable to you as terms you can include in your standard terms and conditions or which you can include in a negotiated contract. Accordingly, using written contracts provides certainty for both the buyer and seller as to their rights and responsibilities and reflects the commercial bargain they have made. Contract terms are discussed in chapter 4.

The Lidl case outlined below demonstrates some of the difficulties that can arise where standard business terms and conditions have not been properly incorporated into the contract between a buyer and a seller.

Case study: Lidl UK GmbH v Hertford Foods Limited and another (2001)

A dispute arose regarding the non-delivery of corned beef by Hertford Foods Limited ('Hertford') under a contract for the supply of the product between Hertford and Lidl UK GmbH ('Lidl'). Hertford stated the non-delivery was due to a shortage of supplies and industrial action in Brazil. Lidl informed Hertford that it would deduct the costs incurred in using alternative suppliers from the payments due to Hertford, as well as withholding payment to cover future potential costs. Lidl also refused to make payment in relation to the deliveries made.

Hertford asserted that its standard terms and conditions applied, cancelled the contract based on Lidl's non-payment and started legal proceedings. Lidl defended the claim, and claimed that its standard terms and conditions applied and its terms allowed the company to withhold payment to cover, the costs incurred, as well as future potential costs. Each set of terms and conditions provided for different remedies in the case of non-delivery and non-payment.

The relationship between the companies first began when a contract for the supply of corned beef was made during a telephone call. There was no discussion regarding contract terms. However, Hertford sent a fax to Lidl after the conversation which included a clause in relation to the payment terms. Evidence was given that Hertford, in accordance with its procedures, also prepared on the same day a standard sales contract confirmation document, which included Hertford's standard conditions of sale. This document was not found on Lidl's files when the matter went to court; however, the court formed the view that it probably arrived at Lidl and that it may have been destroyed when a new member of staff joined who cleared out his predecessor's files. Approximately one month later Lidl, in accordance with its policy, sent a document called a 'quantity contract' confirming the order. This document also stated that Lidl's terms and conditions applied. The terms were stated to be available upon request.

A second order was made by telephone. This was the order which led to the dispute. Hertford sent a fax confirming the order with no mention of Hertford's standard conditions of sale. On the same day, Hertford also prepared its standard sales confirmation document including standard terms of sale, although Lidl denied receiving them. Lidl also sent another 'quantity contract' document to Hertford with the same clause, as referred to above, regarding the application of Lidl's terms and conditions. It was this second order which led to the dispute.

The court found that the representatives of the companies involved in the negotiation of the second order both knew that it was the policy of their respective companies to contract under their own standard conditions. It is not possible to enter into a contract based on both sets of terms. The court decided that the only inference that could be drawn about Hertford's and Lidl's standard terms and conditions was that neither set of terms applied to the contract in relation to the second order. Also, the contract terms which applied were those that had been expressly agreed between Hertford and Lidl or which are implied by law (see page 27 for further information on implied terms).

It also decided, based on general law, that Lidl was entitled to offset the costs incurred in finding an alternative supplier against the money owed to Hertford for the deliveries actually made, but was not entitled to withhold payment against future costs that might be incurred.

If you are using your standard terms and conditions, you need to ensure that they are incorporated into your contract with your client. The Lidl case demonstrates some of the difficulties of just working when there has not been clear acceptance of the terms. Therefore, as suggested above, written acceptance is the best course of action (e.g. in an acceptance form or a signed copy of the terms and conditions).

 The terms of a contract must not be too vague. If they are not clear, it may not be possible to enforce them (see chapter 4 for further information).

Practical tips on standard business terms

- If you are using standard terms and conditions, they need to be properly incorporated into your contracts with your clients or suppliers. You need to bring your terms to the attention of your clients or suppliers.

- To ensure that your contract terms are incorporated into your contracts with your clients or suppliers, do not just state that 'all contracts are subject to our standard terms and are available upon request'. The terms need to be clearly accepted. You should send copies of your terms and this can be easily incorporated into your selling and buying procedures. For example:

- As discussed above, your standard terms can be sent with your proposals to clients for signature.

- Inform your clients that they need to sign and return the signed terms to you before you carry out any work.

- You can also include your standard terms on your business stationery (e.g. on quotation forms, invoices and delivery notes). A statement on the front of the document can be included (e.g. 'All sales are subject to our standard terms and conditions, which are printed on the back of this document'). The size of the font used should be legible.

- It is also customary in standard business terms to include a clause confirming that your terms apply to the contract and supersede any other terms proposed by the client.

- Do not start working if alternative standard terms are proposed or supplied after you have supplied your standard terms. You should respond in writing and confirm that your standard terms apply and that you will not commence work until you have received written confirmation of acceptance. This will make it difficult for your client to argue at a later date that your standard terms do not apply.

Summary of key points

- The basic requirements for the creation of a valid contract are the offer, acceptance, consideration and intention to create legal relations.

- The offer and acceptance must match.

- A response to an offer with changes is not an acceptance. It is a counter-offer. You can choose to accept it, reject it or make a counter-offer.

- The matters agreed during negotiations should be confirmed in writing and included in your contract. Do ensure that you have agreed on all the essential terms.

- Calling a document a 'letter of intent' has no legal meaning. The legal effect (i.e. whether it is legally binding or non-legally binding) of the document will be determined based on the facts.

- If you are working under the standard terms and conditions of another business, make sure that you understand them.

- When using your own standard terms and conditions make sure that they are properly incorporated into the contract.

CHAPTER 4

Contract terms

What you'll find in this chapter
- ✔ Key terms
- ✔ Boiler plate terms
- ✔ Standard terms checklist

Key terms

It is important that you understand the terms of any contract you enter into (irrespective of whether you are buying or selling services or goods). This is because you should understand your rights and obligations. If you do not read the contract and you make a bad deal, you will be stuck with it. There are only a few exceptions where a contract term will be unenforceable (in business-to-business transactions). These will be discussed where relevant in this book; for example, if a clause which excludes liability with regard to breach of contract in a standard set of business terms and conditions is deemed to be unreasonable (we will look at this in more detail below).

Contracts consist of a variety of terms that set out the requirements and obligations of each person who has entered into the contract. Contracts can vary in content and length depending on the complexity and nature of the deal. In this chapter we will look at some of the clauses which are often found in contracts for the supply of goods and/or services.

Parties

You may be familiar with the expression 'parties' in relation to contracts. The parties are those who have entered into the contract. In the context of this book, which focuses on business agreements, the parties will be businesses such as sole traders, companies and partnerships.

 It is important to understand who you are entering into a contract with. It may seem obvious, but if there is a problem such as non-payment or non-performance, you need to know whom to pursue.

You will recall the problems encountered in the Actionstrength case (in chapter 1), i.e. where the person who has guaranteed your payment is not your client and he has not given you a signed written guarantee. You may also recall the example where someone is a director of several companies (please refer to chapter 1). You need to be clear which company the director is representing when he is negotiating and entering into a contract with you, i.e. who the client is.

Full details should be obtained. For example, if it is a company, you must know the full legal name of the company (not just its trading name), business/office address and registered office address. In any event, you can obtain details from Companies House (www.companieshouse.gov.uk). Alternatively, if you are dealing with a partnership or sole trader, you will want similar details for them (e.g. the sole trader's name and not just his trade name). Partnerships and sole traders do not have registered offices.

 It is customary to include definitions in contracts. These are words or expressions which have a specific meaning when used in the contract; for example, "Seller' shall mean Mr Smith'.

Scope of services/work or details of products or goods

This is obviously an essential term of the contract. Each person needs to know what is being supplied. A clear description of the services, work, goods or products needs to be included in the contract. This may be very straightforward if you are selling standard items, such as telephones, shoes or computers.

Alternatively, you may carry out work or provide services which are tailored to the individual requirements of your client or involve various technical aspects; for example, you provide graphic design services, engineering design services or manufacture bespoke products.

This will usually involve putting together a 'scope of services' or 'scope of work' document, which should form part of the contract. This document can include a variety of information. In any event, it should:

- clearly and comprehensively describe the work or services to be provided;

- include any relevant technical specifications or industry standards which may need to be complied with;

- include any special conditions or requirements (e.g. any assumptions made, limitations, special instructions for use of the product or matters which you are not responsible for).

Quality of goods/standard of services

Express terms are often included regarding quality or standards in relation to goods or services. These terms can be included under contract headings known as 'warranties' (referred to below). These terms may also exclude or vary implied terms (e.g. by statute) regarding quality or standards in relation to goods or services supplied in the course of business. You may recall that implied terms were discussed in chapter 3. It is customary in business-to-business contracts to include terms that reflect the exact requirements of the contracting parties, rather than relying on implied terms, which do not always accurately reflect their requirements. Some of the key implied terms are referred to below.

In relation to goods

Satisfactory quality: Goods must be of a satisfactory quality. This means that the goods must be of a standard that a reasonable person would regard as satisfactory. Various matters are considered in assessing satisfactory quality, including the fitness for purpose for which such goods are commonly supplied, description, price, appearance, finish and relevant circumstances.

Fitness for a particular purpose: Goods must be fit for any purpose that your client has made clear to you, or where it should be obvious to you that the goods are wanted for a particular purpose. For example, you sell paint for use on walls and surfaces inside factories and your client makes it clear that he intends to use the paint for the outside of his factory. If you sell the paint to him, the paint must be suitable for exterior use unless you have informed him that you do not believe the paint to be suitable.

In relation to services

Reasonable care and skill: The services must be carried out with reasonable care and skill. If you are supplying services, you do not have to make extraordinary efforts or carry out your services to the 'highest standard' (unless you agree that you will and then you may have difficulty working out what is the highest standard). The level of skill and care will be the standard expected of someone who is a reasonably capable supplier of services in relation to your business or profession.

Warranties

Warranties are often included in contracts and cover a variety of matters; for example, 'The consultant warrants that all services will be carried out with reasonable skill and care' or 'The contractor warrants that all the work produced by him is original and does not infringe any third party's copyright or intellectual property rights'.

You can think of a warranty as a statement or promise about certain conditions or events or actions which are enforceable. Warranties, as with other contract terms, can be implied or expressly included in a contract. Examples of implied warranties are referred to above in the section on 'Quality of goods/standard of services' on page 35.

Sometimes someone does not want to give a warranty so he includes a specific statement to avoid any implication that he may have given a warranty; for example, 'No warranties are given that the software supplied by us is error-free'.

Another example of an exclusion in relation to warranties is set out below:

'Except as specifically stated in clause 3, no warranties or conditions, express or implied (by statute, custom or otherwise), regarding fitness for purpose or satisfactory quality or otherwise, are given in relation to the goods.'

The purpose of such a clause is to make the following clear:

1. Any warranties relating to the goods are in a specific clause (e.g. clause 3). They are not intended to be found in any other part of the contract. This allows the seller to give warranties which are specific to his goods. For example, they might relate to a specific technical specification.

2. No other warranties apply to the goods, including any statutory implied terms, such as the terms as to satisfactory quality and fitness for purpose implied by the Sale of Goods Act 1979 (discussed above). Consideration needs to be given to the requirement for reasonableness (referred to below in 'Limits of liabilities and exclusions') when excluding statutory implied terms.

When including warranties in your contract, do:

•   ensure that you can comply with any warranties you give; and

•   consider (if appropriate) including a clause confirming that all other warranties are excluded except those stated in your contract. You should consider reasonableness requirements as discussed below.

Price

It may seem strange that disputes can arise in relation to price but they occur frequently. Many cases have gone to court where one person believes that they had agreed to carry out work on an hourly-rate basis and the other thinks that it was agreed on a fixed-price basis. If there is no clear agreement as to price, you may find that in the event of a dispute the court will decide that you will be paid a reasonable amount for your work. This is not an ideal situation if your idea of what a reasonable amount is differs from the court's.

You should state:

- the price clearly in your contract;
- whether delivery charges are included or are in addition to the price;
- whether VAT is included or is in addition to the price.

Payment terms

These need to be clearly specified. As previously discussed in chapter 3, consideration needs to be given to your cash flow. Include payment terms which reflect your requirements. You may want to consider including a term in your contract confirming that you have a right to charge interest. You have this right under the Late Payment of Commercial Debts (Interest) Act 2002.

 This legislation applies to business-to-business transactions and allows you to charge interest at eight per cent above the Bank of England base rate.

Payment terms should state the:

- time for payment;
- interest on late payments (as mentioned above, you have this right, but you may want to point it out to your clients);
- time is of the essence in relation to payment.

Time

Time requirements in relation to contract terms or obligations are not automatically regarded as an essential term of the contract. There are some situations where it is usually deemed that 'time will be of the essence' (such as some contracts for the sale of goods where delivery must take place by a fixed time). This means that the time for performing the obligation must be strictly complied with and any failure to comply will be a breach of contract, which can allow the person who has not breached the contract to end the contract and claim damages for the loss that he has suffered due to the breach. To ensure certainty, a party to a contract should specifically state that time is of the essence in relation to a specific requirement; for example, 'Time is of the essence in relation to the delivery of the goods'. You may want to take this approach with your suppliers.

Sometimes it is not possible to commit to a specific time limit. You may confirm that any times given are estimates. A specific term can be included in the contract confirming that time is not of the essence; for example, 'Time is not of the essence for the performance of the services. Any times given in relation to the performance of the services are estimates only'.

Alternatively, it is also possible to agree a time schedule for the performance of the specific contract obligation (e.g. the performance of services or the delivery of goods) and to pay a specified amount as compensation for late performance (and that no other compensation will be payable in relation to late performance). The amount must be a genuine pre-estimate of loss, otherwise it will be regarded as a penalty and unenforceable (due to the legal rules relating to these types of clauses). You should obtain advice in relation to whether such an approach is suitable for you and the drafting of such a clause.

Delivery arrangements, risk and title

In relation to goods, you should have clear terms regarding the delivery arrangements. You should consider various practical issues such as responsibility for loss and damage of goods in transit. Responsibility for loss and damage of goods is often referred to in contracts as 'risk'; for example, 'Risk in goods shall pass to the buyer upon delivery'. This clause means that the responsibility for loss and damage passes from the seller to the buyer at the time the goods are delivered to the buyer.

You should consider taking out appropriate insurance to cover goods in transit. Risk and ownership in goods do not have to pass to the buyer (i.e. your client) at the same time.

It is advisable to retain ownership of the goods until you have received full payment. So, if you deliver the goods before you receive full payment, you should ensure that the risk passes to your client upon delivery, while the ownership remains with you until payment has been received.

Ownership is usually referred to as 'property' or 'title' in contracts; for example, 'Property remains with the seller until payment in full in cleared funds has been received'. The expression 'retention of title clauses' refers to clauses of the type included in the previous example. You should keep these clauses simple unless you have obtained professional advice.

Delivery terms should cover:

- when delivery will be made (where applicable, that the delivery time is an estimate);
- the address to which the goods will be delivered;
- delivery costs;
- whether the buyer is responsible for storage costs in the event that he fails to accept delivery.

Terms dealing with risk and title should cover:

- the responsibility for goods in transit;
- that risk shall pass on delivery;
- that the title remains with the seller until full payment in cleared funds is received.

Confidentiality

Confidentiality can be a sensitive issue. Many contracts contain confidentiality clauses, which require that certain information that has been provided be kept secret. In certain circumstances, the obligation to keep information secret will not apply; for example, where the information is already publicly available or you are legally required to disclose the information; for example, you are required to by a court order.

Intellectual property

As previously discussed in chapter 2, intellectual property rights can be a valuable asset to a business. You are probably familiar with rights such as copyright (which gives you the right to control the copying of your copyrighted works or material), trade marks (which protect your brand or logo) and patents (which can protect your inventions).

Intellectual property rights are a complex subject and a detailed discussion is outside the scope of this book. However, we will look at some of the basic issues which might arise in a supply contract. Your client may want to own the intellectual property rights created in relation to the contract. This is not usually an issue in relation to the sale of physical products (e.g. furniture), where it is normal for the intellectual property rights to remain with the seller. It may arise in relation to services that your client has asked you to carry out specifically for him (e.g. design work or bespoke software design).

 You will need to make a decision as to how you want to deal with intellectual property rights, such as copyright.

Intellectual property rights can be assigned (i.e. transferred) to a client. A copyright assignment must be in writing and signed by the person making the assignment, i.e. the creator of the copyright. Alternatively, you can retain ownership of the copyright and grant a licence to the client. Licences can be exclusive or non-exclusive. An exclusive licence should be in writing and signed by the copyright owner.

Clearly you need to include contract terms that reflect the needs of your business; if you need to use the copyright for future work, do not assign it to your client. For example, the following clause would not be suitable if you wanted to own your copyright as it has the effect of transferring all intellectual property rights to the client:

'All intellectual property rights including, without limitation, copyright, patents, design rights developed by the supplier in carrying out the services shall be assigned to the client.'

Insurance

It may be useful to confirm to a client that you carry relevant insurance. Consider insurance that is applicable to your business, such as professional indemnity and public liability. In any event, some clients may insist that you have insurance and ask for current certificates of insurance to be produced when requested.

Limits of liabilities and exclusions

Liabilities

Liabilities are legal responsibilities. Clauses can be included in contracts describing liabilities that will be accepted and include limits.

Clauses are often included in contracts describing the different types of damage or loss you and your client/supplier shall be responsible for. Here is an example: 'The seller shall be liable for all damage, loss, expenses and claims caused by the seller's breach of contract'. This means that the seller shall be legally responsible for any loss and damage he may cause if he does not comply with his contractual obligations; for example, the seller is required to install a heating system but he installs the system incorrectly which results in a fire. He would be responsible for physical damage, such as loss of property, due to the fire (as this was caused by his defective installation work) and possibly other losses, such as the loss of business or sales due to the buyer not being able to operate his business due to lack of premises.

Rules

It is also possible to limit or exclude liabilities in a contract. Various rules apply in relation to limits or exclusion of liabilities in business-to-business contracts (i.e. written standard terms of business and negotiated contracts). The main rules are set out below:

1. **Personal injury or death:** Liability for personal injury or death caused by negligence cannot be excluded or restricted in a contract.

2. **Negligence (other than negligence which causes personal injury or death):** Contract terms excluding or limiting negligence (e.g. breach of the requirement to carry out services with reasonable care and skill) must comply with the requirements of the reasonableness test (referred to below).

3. **Breach of contract:** Contract terms in your standard written terms of business which exclude or limit liability for breach of contract must satisfy the reasonableness test.

4. **Misrepresentations:** Contract terms excluding or restricting liability for misrepresentations (such as pre-contract statements) must satisfy the reasonableness test.

5. **Statutory implied terms:** Certain statutory implied terms (e.g. satisfactory quality and fitness for purpose) can be excluded or restricted using contract terms to the extent that the contract terms satisfy the reasonableness test. Exclusions relating to the implied term that a person selling goods has the right to sell goods (i.e. the 'title') will be invalid. For example, Clause 6.3 (c) in the sample Sale of Goods contract at the back of the book makes it clear that the limit of liability is not intended to exclude the implied term relating to title (i.e. the reference to Section 12 of the Sale of Goods Act in the clause).

Reasonableness test

A number of factors are considered in establishing reasonableness. They relate to the circumstances at the time the contract was entered into (which were reasonably known or should have been known by the parties). For example, if you include a financial limit in relation to your liability in your standard terms, your available resources to cover your liability and the extent to which you can cover the liability with insurance will be taken into account. If you have a large amount of insurance cover available and a very low contractual limit of liability, the limit may be unreasonable. Other relevant factors which may be taken into account include the bargaining position of you and your client and whether any inducements were given to your client to enter into the contract. In order to establish whether your limits or exclusions of liability in your standard terms and conditions are unreasonable, your client would need to take legal action and the court would then make a decision.

Large companies have often found that the clauses excluding or limiting their liability in their standard terms and conditions are unreasonable and invalid when they have been challenged by court action. A typical example is a company that is a large multinational. It has a large insurance programme to cover its activities and its sales staff pressurise smaller businesses, who may be dependent on or have an urgent need for its products, to sign the company's standard contracts. The sales staff may also make exaggerated claims about the capability of the products they are selling or their ability to comply with their client's time schedule. The smaller companies may find that the multinational's clauses limiting or excluding liability may be found to be unreasonable; for example, a limit of liability which is very low in relation to the risk of loss which can be caused by a breach of contract by the multinational.

This reasonableness test does not apply to the international sale of goods contracts. It should also be noted that liability for fraud cannot be excluded.

Examples

Examples of various typical limitation and exclusion of liability clauses are given below. The need to comply with the reasonableness test should be taken into account (where applicable) if you include similar clauses in your contract.

The purpose of the following limit of liability clause is to set a limit or 'cap' on liability. The clause states the limit does not apply to certain liabilities which cannot legally be excluded (e.g. death due to negligence).

'The Supplier's liability for any damage, loss, claims and expenses caused by the Supplier's services provided under this contract shall not exceed the Contract Price, whether caused by negligence, breach of contract or otherwise, except liability for fraud or for personal injury or death caused by the Supplier's negligence shall not be excluded or restricted'.

Here is an example of a clause where financial losses and certain other losses are not accepted. This is known as an 'exclusion of liability clause': 'We shall not be liable for any loss of profit, revenue, business interruption or indirect or consequential loss, whether caused by negligence, breach of contract or otherwise, except liability for fraud or for personal injury or death caused by our negligence shall not be limited'.

You may see references in contracts to 'consequential' losses or damages. Business people often think that this a way of referring to all types of financial loss, such as loss of profits. They are wrong. Consequential loss is not a legally defined term. While it has no specific meaning, the courts generally regard the term to mean 'indirect losses', that is losses that were not reasonably foreseeable at the time that the contract was entered into as likely to arise from the breach of contract. The general rules regarding compensation for breach of contract are that a person who has entered into a contract should be compensated for losses he has incurred due the other person's breach of contract. These losses are those which were reasonably foreseeable at the time the contract was entered into as being likely to be caused by the breach of contract. He is not entitled to be compensated for losses which were not reasonably foreseeable at the time the contract was entered into as being likely to be caused by the breach of contract (often referred to as indirect losses), unless he has agreed to be compensated for such losses in his contract.

Therefore, if financial loss, such as loss of profit, is caused by your failure to comply with the contract and it was reasonably foreseeable that such loss would have occurred as a result of your failure at the time you entered into the contract, you will be liable unless you included a clause in the contract excluding such liability. Alternatively, you may confirm that you will accept reasonably foreseeable financial losses, but confirm that financial losses that were not reasonably foreseeable are excluded. However, this decision should be made based on the issues which affect your business, such as the nature of the goods and services you provide and the liabilities covered by your insurance. It is advisable to obtain advice in relation to limits of liability and exclusion clauses.

As discussed above, liability for personal injury or death due to negligence or fraudulent misrepresentation cannot be excluded or limited. Therefore, clauses are normally included in contracts that confirm nothing in the contract is intended to exclude such liabilities; for example, 'Nothing in this contract shall exclude or restrict liability for death or personal injury due to negligence or fraudulent misrepresentation'.

Termination and suspension

Termination is not an automatic right for all breaches of contract. Some breaches allow for a contract to be terminated with a right to claim compensation (e.g. a breach of an essential term of the contract), while other breaches of contract give a right to claim for compensation (e.g. a non-essential term). Therefore, it is usual to include termination clauses in contracts, which describe the circumstances in which a contract can be terminated, such as for non-payment and serious breach of contract. Again, the right to suspend the carrying out of a contract is not automatic if there is a breach of contract or dispute. It is worthwhile to consider including a right to suspend the carrying out of a contract if you are not paid on time, which states that you also have no liability regarding such a suspension.

Boiler plate terms

It is usual to include certain standard clauses, such as a Force Majeure, in contracts, which are known as 'boiler plate' terms.

Force Majeure

The purpose of a Force Majeure clause is to confirm that there shall be no breach of contract or liability if an event outside of the control ('Force Majeure') of the parties occurs which causes the affected party or parties to be delayed or prevented from carrying out their obligations.

It is possible that the event can continue for a long period of time, which means that the contract will not be performed. It may not be practical to wait indefinitely for matters to go back to normal. Therefore, it is customary to include a time period which, if exceeded, will allow either party to terminate the contract.

 It is important to describe the meaning of the term 'Force Majeure' in a contract, as it is not a defined term in English and Welsh law.

A simple example of a Force Majeure clause is set out below:

'Neither party will be liable for any failure or delay in performance under this contract to the extent such failure or delay was caused by Force Majeure. For the purposes of this contract, Force Majeure shall mean any event outside of the reasonable control of either party, such as war, flood, government action. The party who is unable to perform or is delayed in his performance must give the other written notification of the Force Majeure as soon as possible after its occurrence. The parties shall try to agree a mutually convenient course of action. If the Force Majeure continues for more than 60 days, either party can terminate this contract with immediate effect by written notice to the other party.'

Examples of other boiler plate terms are set out below:

Assignment

Assignment clauses control the ability of the parties to transfer their rights or benefits under the contract. These rights may include the right to receive payment; for example:

'Neither party to this contract can assign any of their rights under this contract without the consent of the other party, which shall not be unreasonably withheld.'

Subcontracting

Clauses are often included by clients restricting their suppliers' right to subcontract work. If there is no express restriction in your contract, there is nothing to prevent you from entering into a subcontract. However, you may prefer to include an express statement confirming that you have a right to subcontract work; for example, 'The supplier reserves the right to subcontract any of its obligations under this contract'.

Waiver

The purpose of a waiver clause is to confirm that if there is a delay in enforcing a legal right, that the right is not lost if it is used at a later date. Here is an example clause:

'The failure of any party to this contract to exercise or enforce any right hereunder shall not be deemed to constitute a waiver of that right nor operate to prevent the exercise of such right at any time thereafter.'

Third-party rights

This clause means that only the people who enter into the contract have the right to have any benefit from the contract or enforce it. An example clause is below:

'No-one who is not a party to this contract has any benefit or any right to enforce any term of this contract for the purposes of the Contracts (Rights of Third Parties) Act 1999.'

Entire agreement

The main purpose of an entire agreement clause is to make sure all the terms of the deal are contained in the written contract. This means that no related verbal discussions are intended to form part of the contract. A statement can be included which confirms that there shall be no liability for statements made before the contract (except fraudulent misrepresentations) and they are not part of the contract. Statements may have been made during negotiations or included in advertising material (see chapter 2 for further information). However, the requirements of the reasonableness test should be taken into account. Also, confirmation can be included that changes to the contract can only be made in writing by authorised representatives.

An example

1. This Agreement contains the entire agreement and understanding between the parties relating to the subject matter of this Agreement and supersedes all prior agreements and understandings (whether oral or in writing).

2. Each party acknowledges that they are not relying on any statements, warranties or representations given or made by the other party except as expressly set out in this Agreement. Nothing in this clause shall, however, operate to limit or exclude any liability for fraudulent misrepresentation.

3. Variations to this Agreement can only be made in writing by the agreement of the parties and signed by their authorised representatives.

Applicable law and dispute resolution

The purpose of this clause is to confirm which country's laws shall apply to the contract (e.g. in relation to interpretation) as well as how and where disputes will be resolved. If you and your client are both based in England, you will usually want the laws of England and Wales to apply. You may also agree that disputes can only be referred to English and Welsh courts (as opposed to another country's courts or another method of resolving disputes as discussed in chapter 8). For example:

'The laws of England and Wales shall apply to this contract, and the parties accept the exclusive jurisdiction of the English and Welsh courts.'

However, if you have an overseas client, he may be reluctant to agree to English and Welsh law. He may prefer the laws of his own country and have disputes resolved by his country's courts. This might not suit you. You need to consider various commercial and practical issues. For example, you need to understand how foreign laws affect your contract. Other considerations include starting legal proceedings in another country and the legal costs (e.g. documents may need to be translated) and how you manage your relationship with an overseas lawyer (regular visits may not be practical). You need to agree a suitable position. Various options are available, such as arbitration, which is an alternative to court proceedings. Arbitration is discussed in chapter 8. Obtain advice to assist you in making a decision.

Standard terms checklist

When considering the matters which should be included in your standard terms for your business, you will find that the process will help you think about many practical issues and how you want to deal with them. The checklist below provides some basic items you may want to consider in relation to your standard contract terms. This is not an exhaustive or exclusive list.

Scope of services/deliverables/goods

Have you included a description of the services or goods, or a detailed scope of the work? ☐

Standard of service/quality of goods

Have you inserted the appropriate warranties regarding standards and quality? ☐

Have you considered including an exclusion clause which confirms that no other warranties are given except as expressly stated in the contract? ☐

Price and payment terms

Have you included the details of the price (including whether it is inclusive of VAT) and payment terms (e.g. advance payment, payment with 14 days of date of invoices)? ☐

Delivery arrangements for goods

Have you inserted the delivery arrangements for the goods? ☐

Risk and ownership of goods

Have you inserted terms confirming:

- that risk passes on delivery? ☐

- the position regarding risk in relation to goods during transit? ☐

- that the title shall pass on payment? ☐

Time-related obligations

If you do not want time to be of the essence, have you specified and stated that any quotations regarding time are estimates? ☐

Intellectual property

If applicable, have you included a term dealing with the ownership of intellectual property rights which are appropriate to your contract and business? ☐

Liability

Have you considered including a limitation of liability clause? ☐

Have you taken into account the reasonableness requirements? ☐

Have you obtained advice in relation to limitations and exclusion of liabilities? ☐

Events outside of your control

Have you included a Force Majeure clause to cover possible delays or non-performance due to events outside of your control? ☐

Termination and suspension

Have you considered the circumstances in which you will
want to terminate the contract (e.g. serious breach of contract
or convenience, i.e. where there is no fault)? ☐

Have you ensured that you have a right to receive payment for
the work carried out until termination? ☐

Have you included the right to terminate the contract in the
event of non-payment? ☐

Special requirements

Do you have any special requirements which should be
included in the contract? ☐

Boiler plate clauses

Have you included boiler plate clauses? ☐

CHAPTER 5

E-commerce

The internet has had a massive impact on business. The usual legal rules apply when selling goods or services over the internet. However, there are additional practical and legal issues which need to be considered. This chapter looks at selling over the internet in the context of business-to-business transactions.

There are additional rules which apply when selling to consumers, i.e. individuals who are not acting in a business capacity, but this is outside the scope of this book. However, if you are interested, you can obtain fact sheets and useful information from the Department of Trade and Industry's (DTI) website regarding distance selling and e-commerce in relation to consumers at www.dti.gov.uk/ccp/topics1/ecomm.htm. You should also obtain advice if you intend to sell to consumers online.

This chapter focuses on the following issues:

- Your website and content

- E-commerce regulations

- Contract formation

- Data protection
- Website terms and policies

Your website and content

You can spend a lot of time developing your website. For example, you may want to make sure that it easy to use and attractive to look at. Functionality and appearance are important. However, you should also ensure that the legal issues are properly dealt with in relation to setting up your website and the content that you intend to use.

Your domain name

The first thing you need to do is buy the domain name. The domain name is the name you use for your website, such as www.lawpack.co.uk. Usually, you will buy the domain name which is the same as your company name.

Alternatively, you may want to buy a different name. You should carry out various checks to ensure that you do not use a name which is a registered trade mark or is currently being used by another business. If you use a registered trade mark or a business name (which is not a registered trade mark), you can face legal action. Business names which are not registered as a trade mark can be protected by a legal action known as 'passing off'. This legal action protects one business from having its services or products represented as the services or products of another business. You should obtain advice if you are facing potential legal action regarding the use of a business name or if you discover that someone is using your business name.

You can carry out searches including:

- the Patent Office (www.patent.gov.uk) for registered trade marks;
- Companies House (www.companieshouse.gov.uk) for company names and limited liability partnership names;
- business and trade directories;
- the internet.

In the event of a domain name dispute, it is possible to resolve some disputes without going to court. Disputes regarding domain names, such as abusive registrations, can be resolved in accordance with the ICANN (Internet Corporation for Assigned Names and Numbers) dispute resolution policies; for example, in relation to .com, .net and .org domain names. Nominet also has a dispute resolution procedure in relation to .uk domain names. These dispute procedures are a much cheaper alternative than legal proceedings in the court. ICANN (www.icann.org) is responsible for co-ordination and management of the domain name system and Nominet (www.nominet.org.uk) is the registry for .uk domain names. Therefore, if you find out that someone has deliberately registered your business name or trade mark as a domain name, you may want to consider using these dispute resolution procedures. Powers exist to cancel, suspend or transfer domain names. You should check the specific rules for the details of eligibility for dealing with claims and current costs.

Your website content

There are some intellectual property issues you need to consider when putting together the content of your website. Intellectual property rights are discussed in chapter 4. They are relevant in relation to your website content and the development of your website. People often think that if they find photographs or articles on the internet then they can simply use them for their commercial purposes. This is not the case.

Intellectual property rights

Copyright exists in relation to relevant works (e.g. literary, musical, artistic and dramatic works) as soon as they are created. Copyright gives the owner the right to copy the relevant work/materials, as well as certain other rights. There are no registration requirements for copyright to exist. You need to consider the types of work and materials you may use in relation to your website. For example, videos, music, e-books, articles, photographs, text and images are all protected by copyright.

In relation to the source of the material, you may be paying people to develop content for your website (e.g. designing graphics, taking photographs or creating databases) and you will want to own the copyright as well as the database right (which is an intellectual property right which protects databases). You may recall from chapter 2 that the creator of copyright is the owner unless otherwise agreed (or where the creator is an employee in which case it belongs to his employer). Therefore, you should ensure that the copyright is assigned upon creation, i.e. a written agreement signed by the creator. The position with databases is a little unclear – therefore the safest position is to ensure that the creator of the database also enters into a signed written agreement.

 In addition to copyright and database rights, there are other intellectual property rights that you may need to consider, such as trade marks.

Metatags

Metatags are invisible words that are hidden in a website. These words are used to describe services or website content so that the website can be found by search engines.

 Don't be tempted to use competitors' trade marks and business names in your metatags in an attempt to get more people to visit your website. You could end up facing legal action (e.g. a trade mark infringement).

Advertising

Advertising is regulated by a variety of legislation. Some relate to specific products or services. Advice should be sought in relation to your specific business. UK advertisers are required to comply with the British Code of Advertising, Sales Promotion and Direct Marketing. Adverts should be lawful, decent and truthful. Details can be found on the Advertising Standards Authority's (ASA) website at www.asa.org.uk/asa/codes.

Links

It is good practice to request permission from another website owner before you link to his website. You may also want to make it clear on your website that links to your website require your permission.

Practical tips

In relation to the information, material and other content you use for your website, you should:

- Get written permission for the use of any material or content (e.g. text, photographs) that you do not own.

- Use written signed contracts with anyone who is working on or developing material or content for your website dealing with ownership of copyright and other intellectual property rights. You should also obtain confirmation that the content or material he supplies does not infringe any third-party intellectual property rights.

- Avoid other people's business names or trade marks in your metatags.

- Include a copyright notice on your website confirming ownership of your copyright.

Your website developer

You should enter into a written contract, as discussed above, with your website developer dealing with ownership of copyright and other intellectual property rights in relation to the website. Usually, you will be interested in owning the rights in the 'front-end' of the website, not the 'back-end' (e.g. the operating software or coding that he needs to use with other customers).

E-Commerce Regulations

The Electronic Commerce (EC Directive) Regulations 2002 ('E-Commerce Regulations') apply to most UK commercial websites including websites which do not sell online. You can obtain a copy of the regulations online at Her Majesty's Stationery Office at www.legislation. hmso.gov.uk/si/si2002/20022013.htm.

The regulations also apply to other activities (e.g. selling by interactive television) and the liabilities of internet service providers. However, this chapter will focus on selling online.

Some of the key areas to which the E-Commerce Regulations apply are:

- The supply of information
- The electronic formation of contracts
- Applicable law

Supply of information

Website owners (who advertise their products or services online) and businesses which trade online must provide certain business information. These service providers must provide the information in a form which is easily, directly and permanently accessible (i.e. included on your website). The information to be supplied is the service provider's details:

- Name – the full legal name of the business (and any trade names should be provided to avoid any confusion as to the identity and name of the business).
- Geographical address where the service provider is established.
- VAT number (if registered).
- Contact details which allow rapid communication, including an email address.
- Details of registration in a trade register, such as the name of the register and registration number (if applicable). These registers relate to the service being provided and not the general business of the service provider.
- Details of the service provider's regulated profession (if the business is part of a regulated profession) including his professional title and the applicable professional rules and details of where to find the rules.
- Details of any authorisation scheme which relate to the service being provided (if applicable).
- References to prices should be clear and unambiguous and should state whether they are inclusive of taxes and delivery charges.

The electronic formation of contracts

The information referred to below needs to be provided before a contract can be concluded electronically (e.g. over the internet) unless parties who are not consumers (e.g. businesses) agree otherwise.

The following information needs to be provided in a clear, comprehensive and unambiguous manner before an order is made:

- The different technical steps to conclude the contract stages (so that it is clear when a legally-binding contract is made).

- The technical means to identify and correct any errors which have been input before an order is made. For example, a page can be included on your website which asks buyers to confirm that their business details and the details of their order are correct before they place the order. If the order or their details need to be changed, they can be directed back to the previous pages and provided with information as to how they can make the necessary amendments.

- The languages offered for the conclusion of the contract.

- Details of whether the contract will be filed and if it will be accessible. (Filing is not defined in the E-Commerce Regulations. Therefore, the DTI has provided guidance that 'filing' is a non-UK-legal concept which does not usually apply within the UK except where a contract is made with a service provider based in an EEA country. The EEA consists of the EU countries plus Iceland, Norway and Liechtenstein.)

Details of any applicable code of conduct which is subscribed to must also be provided and how to access them electronically.

Orders placed by technological means must be acknowledged electronically (e.g. by email or onscreen) without any undue delay. However, if the parties are non-consumers (e.g. businesses), they can agree that the requirements in relation to the acknowledgement of the order and any applicable codes are not applicable.

The terms and conditions in relation to the contract must also be available in a form that the buyer can store and reproduce (e.g. on a printed delivery note).

Applicable law

A business established in the UK which has an online business must comply with the laws of the UK, irrespective of whether goods or services are supplied in the UK or EEA. There are some exceptions to this rule – one important exception is regarding consumers. This means UK online businesses which supply to consumers in the EEA must comply with the relevant countries' consumer laws.

Forming contracts over the internet

Forming contracts over the internet has been discussed in relation to the E-Commerce Regulations. It is useful to look at this in further detail. You may recall cases where large companies had underpriced their products on their websites and they were obliged to sell at the wrong price; for example, vacuum cleaners which should have been sold at £200 were sold at £20. This is because they had entered into a legally binding contract and had to sell the products at the incorrect price.

You may recall from chapter 3 that the basic requirements for a valid contract are the offer, acceptance, intention to create legal relations and consideration. In relation to selling over the internet, when a buyer places an order online this is an offer to buy. The problems above occurred because the companies had structured their websites to accept immediately offers to buy their products (at this point they had formed a contract).

It is important that you structure your website and the contract formation process so that you are not obliged to sell your goods when you do not want to; for example, where your goods are incorrectly priced or out of stock.

An example of an order process is set out below:

- Make it clear to the buyer that his order is an offer to buy.

- A buyer should be required to confirm the acceptance of your terms of sale before he makes an order (e.g. to tick a box with 'I accept').

- Acknowledge the order (e.g. via email or on the web page). You can confirm that the order is being processed and that a legally binding contract will not be concluded until his order has been accepted. This gives you time to check availability, check the item is correctly priced and that there has been no problem with payment before you accept the order (i.e. the offer to buy).

- Regarding the acceptance of the order, you need to decide when you will accept the buyer's order (i.e. the offer) and then notify him of the acceptance. This could be after the payment has cleared.

 This information regarding the contracting formation process can be included in the terms and conditions of sale.

Data protection

Businesses that handle personal data are required to register (also known as 'notification') with the Information Commissioner (www.information commissioner.gov.uk) unless they are exempt. Details of the limited exemptions can be found on the Information Commissioner's website. Personal data can be collected in various ways, such as through forms completed over the internet, as well as records kept about employees, clients or suppliers who are sole traders or partnerships. Personal data must be used fairly and lawfully, in addition to various other requirements which must be complied with which are known as the 'principles of data protection'.

 The Information Commissioner has issued detailed guidance on the principles of data protection which can be found on its website.

Website terms and policies

Depending on the nature of your business and content of your website, you will need to have various terms and policies for your website. Typically, websites will have the following:

1. **Terms of use**

    These terms will set out the basis upon which the site can be used. They may contain:

    - details of the owner of the website;

    - clauses confirming the ownership of intellectual property;

    - exclusions of liability arising out of the use of any information on the website;

    - exclusions of liability regarding any inaccurate information that may be on the website;

    - clauses confirming that no guarantee is given that access to the website will be uninterrupted and exclusions regarding liability due to non-availability/interruption of access to the website.

2. **Terms and conditions of sale**

    These terms will contain the terms and conditions relating to the sale of the goods or the services via the website. Sometimes the general terms of use and terms of sale are combined to form one set of terms.

3. **Privacy policy**

    The privacy policy should contain details about the reasons for collecting personal data and the purposes for which they will be used. The OECD (Organisation For Economic Co-operation and Development) has provided a free privacy policy-generator which can be used to assist putting together privacy policies (www.oecd.org/sti/privacygenerator). Information about the use of cookies is usually included in the privacy policy. Cookies are pieces of information which are stored on the computers of visitors to websites. You are required to inform users if your website uses cookies and how they can reject them. Useful information, including example cookie policies, can be found on www.allaboutcookies.org.

Summary of key points

- Carry out checks before selecting your domain name.

- Do not use content which is unlawful or infringes any third-party intellectual property rights.

- Use written signed contracts with third parties you have engaged to carry out work which deals with ownership of intellectual property rights.

- Comply with the E-Commerce Regulations.

- Ensure that you have a clear process for contracting over the internet.

- Suitable terms and policies should be included on your website.

CHAPTER 6

Selling overseas

What you'll find in this chapter

✔ Getting advice
✔ Doing business overseas

Selling your products to foreign markets can provide you with significant financial benefits. However, poor planning and mistakes can cost you a lot of money.

This chapter will look at some of the basic issues associated with selling overseas. Due to the varying customs, practices and legal issues throughout the world, this chapter is not intended to provide a comprehensive analysis of all the relevant issues (selling over the internet has been looked at in chapter 5), but it is a general overview of some of the basic matters to be considered when selling overseas.

Getting advice

If you have no experience of selling your products or services overseas and you would like to develop your business in this direction, you should first obtain advice from experienced professionals (e.g. lawyers, tax and finance advisers, etc.). A useful starting point is UK Trade & Investment (www. uktradeinvest.gov.uk). This government organisation provides support, advice and assistance to UK businesses that want to develop their business on an international basis. It can provide practical and financial support. You may also want to consider local business support organisations, such as your local Chamber of Commerce, that often provide advice and training in relation to businesses involved in exporting.

Doing business overseas

There are various methods which can be used when selling overseas. These may involve selling direct from the UK to overseas businesses. You may work with multinational clients which involve you negotiating contracts in the UK and providing services or supplying products to them overseas. You may decide to expand your operations by setting up a branch office or company in another country. Alternatively, you may decide that you will use a distributor or an agent with local knowledge of the relevant country. A detailed discussion regarding agency and distribution agreements is outside of the scope of this book. However, in simple terms, an agent acts on behalf of a supplier (e.g. he negotiates the sale on behalf of the supplier). A distributor buys goods or products from a supplier then sells them to his customers.

You should obtain advice to assist you in selecting a method of selling or doing business overseas which is most appropriate for your business.

Export licences

You may find that in some situations your ability to export certain types of goods is restricted or requires an export licence. The restrictions or licence requirements that apply depend on the type of goods (e.g. often relating to technology or goods that are capable of having a military purpose in addition to a commercial purpose) as well as the end-user or country to which the goods are intended to be exported.

 Full details of export control requirements and sanctions can be found on the Department of Trade and Industry's website at www.dti.gov.uk/export.control.

Compliance with overseas laws

If you are selling directly to clients overseas or plan to open a branch office or establish yourself overseas, you should obtain advice from experts on the relevant country's legal and tax issues. For example, are there any specific formalities or filing requirements regarding contracts or registration, or are there any specific safety requirements you need to comply with? Advice should be obtained regarding any laws which apply to agency and distributor relationships in the country where the agents or distributors are based or carrying out their activities.

Contracts

Your standard business terms which you use in the UK may not be suitable for overseas transactions. You should have them reviewed by a lawyer and amended for use overseas. Many UK law firms have branches overseas or relationships with foreign firms that they can refer you to. Details of how to find a UK lawyer can be found in chapter 9. Alternatively, you may need to have specific terms drawn up. Also, see below regarding the use of Incoterms in international contracts for the sale of goods.

Price and payment

You should make sure that your price includes all the relevant taxes and costs. Specify the currency you want to get paid in. Confusion can often arise on this point. The ideal situation is to receive payment in the currency in which the price is specified (i.e. the price is stated in Pound Sterling (£) and payment is received in Pound Sterling (£)).

If you are willing to accept payment in a currency other than Pound Sterling (£), you will need to consider the foreign exchange rate. For example, you specify a price at the time you enter into the contract in Pound Sterling of £1,000 for your work. You agree to accept payment in US Dollars from your client. At the time your client enters into the contract the exchange rate is £1:US$1.5; therefore, the price in Dollars at that time is $1,500. By the time you have carried out the work, the exchange rate has changed to £1:US$1.80. Therefore, the amount payable by your client is now $1,800 (as the price is £1,000). No discussions took place regarding the exchange rate at the time the contract was entered into. Your client wants to pay you $1,500 because that was the value in Dollars of £1,000 when you entered into the contract. You want to be paid $1,800 because after the Dollars have been converted to Pounds that equals £1,000.

To avoid this type of problem, the best course of action is to receive payment in the currency in which the price is specified. This means any risk of changes of foreign exchange rate stay with your client. If you are willing to accept payment in a foreign currency, you will want to minimise the risk of changes in foreign exchange rate risks. You may want to do this by specifying that the payment of the price is based on the exchange rate at a specified point (e.g. the date of the invoice or date of payment). There is still some risk that there can be a change, however, due to electronic banking. There should only be a short period of time between the date of invoice/date of payment is made and the date that you receive payment.

You should also find out if there are any foreign exchange restrictions in your client's country, as you will want to get paid in hard currency or a currency which can be converted.

Incoterms

The International Chamber of Commerce has developed standard terms for use in international contracts for sale of goods, known as 'Incoterms'. These terms are defined to cover the responsibilities of the buyer and the seller in relation to delivery arrangements, import and export costs, passing of risk and insurance. These terms are usually referred to by an abbreviation consisting of three letters, such as 'FOB'. FOB means free on board. This Incoterm is used in relation to contracts for sale where the goods will be transported by ship. The term means that the goods will be deemed to be delivered when they have passed the ship's rail at the port named in the contract (e.g. FOB (Southampton)). At that point, the buyer will be responsible for any loss or damage to the goods. The seller is also responsible for taking the necessary action to clear the goods for export.

Incoterms are regularly used in international sales contracts as they are understood throughout the world. They also reduce the risk of misunderstanding between contracting parties from different countries who may have differing practices and customs in relation to non-international sales. You should always use the most current edition of the Incoterms. The current version is 'Incoterms 2000'. Full details about Incoterms, including where they can be purchased, can be found on the International Chamber of Commerce's website at www.iccwbo.org/index_incoterms.asp.

Insurance and finance

You should check to see whether your current insurance arrangements cover your overseas activities. You may need additional insurance.

UK exporters can also obtain financial products from the Export Credits Guarantee Department (ECGD). ECGD schemes and products are subject to certain eligibility criteria (e.g. exporters who work under short-term credit arrangements are not eligible). You should check the details of the relevant product and eligibility criteria on its website at www.ecgd.gov.uk.

Brand and product protection

If you plan to expand your business and sell your products or services overseas, you should consider taking steps to protect your brand and product in the country where you will be selling. You can do this by registering relevant intellectual property rights, such as patents and trade marks.

 Trade marks provide protection in the country where they are registered. You should obtain advice from a specialist in the relevant country's laws.

A Community Trade Mark (CTM) registration can be made which covers all EU countries. The Patent Office (www.patent.gov.uk) has issued guidance on the CTM and the application process which can be found on its website at www.patent.gov.uk/tm/info/comutm.pdf.

You may also want to consider making an application for a registered design, if relevant to your product. A registered design is an intellectual property right which relates to the appearance of a product. As with the CTM, an application for a registered design can be made which covers all EU countries (Registered Community Designs). The Patent Office has issued guidance on the application process which can be found on its website at www.patent.gov.uk/design/info/comdes.pdf.

Applications in relation to CTMs and Registered Community Designs can be made directly to the Office for Harmonization in the Internal Market (Trade Marks and Design) (OHIM) in Alicante, Spain or through the UK Patent Office. The OHIM website is oami.eu.int.

 Applications for the registration of trade marks and registered designs covering the UK are made to the Patent Office.

Your goods may qualify for patent protection. International applications can be made. See the Patent Office's website for details.

You should also include copyright notices on your copyrighted work or materials (e.g. manuals, books, DVDs, software); for example, © A Company Limited 2005.

Supply of personnel

If your business involves sending people overseas to supply services (e.g. consultancy, training or maintenance services), you will need to consider issues such as work permits and tax. Depending on the duration of the visit to the country, there may be local tax liabilities associated with the personnel.

Taxes and duties: Consideration will need to be given to taxes and duties which may be payable in the countries where you are selling your products/services (e.g. local taxes, import taxes and duties). These costs should be included in your prices where applicable.

Summary of key points

- Obtain professional advice before selling overseas (e.g. in relation to legal and tax issues).

- Check to see if there any restrictions or licence requirements in relation to technology or equipment that you are intending to export.

- Protect your brand and products by registering intellectual property rights where applicable.

- Use contracts which are appropriate for overseas transactions. Obtain advice from a lawyer.

- Review your current insurance arrangement.

- Ensure that all relevant costs are included in your prices. Obtain payment in Pound Sterling. If you are willing to accept payment in foreign currency, you need to minimise the risk of changing foreign exchange rates. Get paid in a hard currency or convertible currency.

CHAPTER 7

The performance of the contract

What you'll find in this chapter

✔ Your obligations
✔ Variations/changes
✔ Suppliers/subcontractors

After you have entered into a contract with your client, it is time to get on with supplying your goods or services that have been agreed with him. This chapter looks at some of the practical issues when carrying out your contract.

Your obligations

Your contract should not dominate your relationship with your client. You need to get on with the practicalities of running your business and supplying goods or services. However, it is important that you understand your contractual obligations as well as your rights. Many businesses get into problems because they do not comply with their obligations or do not fully understand the terms of their contract. A contract is not a one-sided relationship; your client also has to comply with his obligations. Make sure you understand what is required of you and him. Chapter 4 discusses some of the terms which are typically found in contracts for the supply of goods and/or services.

Variations/changes

Once work has started under a contract, you or your client may find that changes need to be made. These may be technical or commercial/legal changes. Before changes are made, it is important to first check to see whether there is a specific procedure for making changes in your contract. Alternatively, it may simply be a case of having a discussion with your client and agreeing the changes in writing. You should not simply go ahead and make changes to the services or goods you are supplying unless you have a contractual right to make changes without the consent of your client (which does not occur very often).

 If you go ahead and make changes without agreement, you could find yourself in the position of being in a dispute or having to carry out additional work for free!

In the event that you need to make a change or your client requests a change:

- Check if there is a contract change procedure and follow the procedure or discuss and agree the changes.

- Record the agreed changes in writing, which should be signed by the parties to the contract. This document should also confirm that the terms and conditions of the contract still apply.

- Changes (e.g. technical ones or changing the scope of the services or work, or the time for the performance) usually involve adjusting the price, so also do not forget to agree and record any price change.

- Do not start work until the changes have been agreed and documented.

Suppliers/subcontractors

If you are using key suppliers/subcontractors who you are dependent on to carry out work for your client or supply products to him, you need to manage these relationships effectively.

One of the first things you need to do is to put contracts in place with your suppliers and subcontractors (if you have not already done this). You should check that there are no restrictions on subcontracting and obtain consent if necessary. Depending on the nature of your business and the extent to which you depend on your supplier/subcontractor, you should consider entering into a contract which passes on the key requirements in your contract with your client into your contract with your supplier/subcontractor.

Ideally, if you have a major or complex contract with your client, you should negotiate with your key suppliers/subcontractors at the same time. In the event that you come across some difficult issues in relation to your client contract negotiations, you can simultaneously deal with these in your supplier/subcontractor negotiations. Otherwise, you may find yourself in a position where you have signed a contract with a client and are having to approach key suppliers/subcontractors who may not be willing to do business on similar terms to those you have with your client.

In the event that you have to rely on key suppliers/subcontractors:

- Enter into written contracts with them that are consistent with the terms of your client contract – for major or complex client contracts, consider negotiating these contracts at the same time as the client contract.

- Regularly monitor the progress of their work.

- Obtain copies of their insurance policies or certificates of insurance (and include a right requiring them to produce insurance documents in their contracts).

- Remind them of any confidentiality obligations which may be applicable.

Insurance

Most businesses carry insurance to cover their activities and legal obligations. If it is a requirement of your contract that you have to carry certain insurance or provide certificates of insurance, you should comply with these obligations. In the course of performing your contract, if there are any matters which may lead to a claim on your insurance policy (e.g. a dispute with a client), you should notify your insurers (see chapter 8 for more information).

 If your business activities have changed since you first obtained your insurance, you should inform your insurers to ensure that all the work you carry out for your clients is covered.

Communications

You should ensure that your staff who are involved with carrying out work for your client understand the key requirements of your contract.

Email is an effective business tool. However, the informality of emails can lead to problems with internal and external business communications. If you have concerns regarding the communication of confidential matters, you may need to consider an alternative form of communication or use some form of security technology. To avoid inadvertently agreeing to contract changes, you may want to make it clear that it is not your policy to conclude contractual arrangements via email. You can include a standard disclaimer in your emails; for example, 'It is the policy of our company not to conclude contracts via email. Nothing in this email shall be regarded as forming a contract or varying any existing contract to which this email may relate'.

It is quite easy to make comments or statements in internal correspondence, such as by email or a confidential internal memo, which has not been fully considered and which you may regret at a later date. Remarks or statements which are admissions of fault or problems, or are construed as admissions, are often found in internal communication documents and emails. These often come to light when there is a dispute that goes to court and which involves the disclosure of documents that are relevant to the dispute. This matter is discussed in further detail in chapter 8.

In relation to the performance of your contract, it is always good practice:

- to brief, where applicable, your key staff on the contract requirements as well as having regular project team meetings to review progress;

- to avoid using emails for confidential communications;

- to consider the statements you make in internal communications and obtain appropriate advice before you make an admission.

Summary of key points

- Ensure that you understand your contractual obligations and comply with them.

- Know your contractual rights.

- Changes, including price, should be agreed in writing and signed by the contract parties.

- Use written contracts with your suppliers and subcontractors.

- Key requirements in your client contracts should be reflected in your supplier/subcontractor contracts.

- Ensure that your insurers have an up-to-date description of the work that you carry out for your clients.

- Include disclaimers in emails if you do not intend to enter into legally-binding contracts by email.

CHAPTER 8

Dealing with disputes

What you'll find in this chapter

✔ The first steps
✔ Legal remedies
✔ Compensation
✔ Legal action
✔ Alternative dispute resolution

Ideally, you will have carried out your contract without any problems. If you do find yourself in the unfortunate situation where you have to deal with complaints or a potential legal claim from your client or supplier, you need to know how to deal with the situation. This chapter focuses on dealing with disputes.

The first steps

There are a number of practical steps you need to take when you are faced with an unhappy client or supplier making a complaint or threatening to take you to court.

Don't panic!

This may seem obvious, but just because someone claims you have caused a problem it does not mean that you are the cause. In business disputes, many factors and people can contribute to a problem. If various businesses are involved on a project, it is not always a clear-cut case of one business being at fault. Sometimes several businesses can jointly cause a problem, therefore they can be jointly responsible. The matter needs to be investigated, which brings us to the next point below.

Get the facts

Ensure you obtain the details of your client's or supplier's complaint. You need to investigate fully his complaint and gather information. Get your contract and have a look at it to see if you have complied with all your obligations and check to see if your client or supplier has complied with his. You should also gather notes of any meetings, emails and documentation relating to the contract and complaint. Speak to your staff who were involved in carrying out the work or supplying your products. If this matter ends up going to court, you will need to gather this information. You will also be required to disclose relevant documentation (including documents which support the claimant's case) if the matter goes to court, except documents which are subject to 'legal privilege' (see below).

Be careful what you say

You may not be prepared when you receive an unexpected telephone call from an angry client or supplier, but you should try to avoid inadvertently saying things you may regret at a later date.

For example, a company receives a telephone call from a client complaining that the quality of the work carried out by one of its employees is poor and does not meet the standards specified in the contract. The manager who receives the telephone call says to the client, 'I am really sorry. The person who carried out the work is a junior employee who is new to the company and I know that he needs more supervision'. This is definitely not a good response. In effect, the manager has said that an inexperienced member of staff carried out the work and he was not properly supervised. The manager has not obtained all the relevant facts. He has not established whether the work has actually been carried out to a poor standard. The manager has assumed the client is correct, whereas the employee may have carried out the work properly. Alternatively, if there is a problem, it may have been caused or contributed to by someone else. However, he has indicated that the work was probably not carried out with reasonable care and skill and the company was at fault.

 Cases are often damaged by comments found in internal documents (e.g. in emails or internal memos). Marking internal documentation 'confidential' will not protect documents from being disclosed in legal proceedings. You should obtain legal advice before making any admissions.

Your insurer will also want to make sure that you do not make any admission without his advice. Admissions made without the advice of your insurer may result in you not being able to make a claim on your insurance. It is a usual condition of insurance policies that insurers should be notified of any potential claim and no admissions should be made without their input.

Contact your insurer and lawyer

As stated above, you should notify your insurer of any issue which may result in you having to make a claim. In any event, you should check the terms of your insurance policy to find out if it covers any loss or damage you are alleged to have caused. Most insurance policies have a number of exclusions. Unfortunately, most people do not realise that some matters are not covered until they have to make a claim. It is a good idea to familiarise yourself with the terms of your policy when you take out or renew your insurance. In any event, when you do so, you should make your requirements and details of your business clear to your insurance broker. You should also consider drafting your business's contract terms so that they are consistent with the liabilities covered by your insurance (e.g. its liability and indemnity clauses).

Communications between you and your lawyer are protected by a special type of confidentiality called 'legal privilege'. This means that privileged communications (e.g. letters, emails, etc.) between you and him are generally protected from being disclosed. Documents protected by legal privilege are usually protected from being disclosed in court.

The subject of legal privilege is complex. Therefore, in the event of a dispute you should consult your solicitor who can discuss this matter with you in further detail and give you advice.

Negotiation

You should always try to see if you can resolve the matter without having to resort to legal action. Look at the practical steps you can take to negotiate a solution to the problem. In the event that this is not possible, you will need to understand the legal remedies which are available.

Legal remedies

In the event of disputes, you should first have a look at your contract to see what rights and remedies you have, as well as the rights and remedies of the other contracting party (e.g. your client or supplier).

Your contract

Your contract may contain rights to suspend or terminate the contract. If these rights are contained in the contract, you should follow the procedures contained in it. For example, you may have a right to terminate for a material breach of an obligation by giving seven days' written notice. If you do not follow the stated procedure, you may find that you have not effectively terminated your contract.

If you decide to terminate, you will want to receive payment for the work you performed before termination. If your relationship with your client has broken down and he is refusing to comply with his payment obligations, you will need to take legal action to enforce your rights.

General law

If you do not have a written contract or a contract which does not deal with rights of termination, you will need to look at general law. If there has been a breach of contract, there is not an automatic right of termination in relation to all breaches.

A basic summary of the position regarding the general law in relation to rights of termination and compensation is set out below.

1. The person who has not breached the contract can always claim damages (i.e. compensation) for the losses that he incurs due to the other contract party's failure to comply with his contractual obligations (i.e. his breach of contract).

2. There is no automatic right to terminate the contract due to the other party's breach of contract. The right to terminate applies in certain situations (see below).

3. In the event of a breach of a major contract term or a very serious breach of contract (i.e. where a person refuses to carry out the contract or shows that it is his intention not to carry it out), the person who is not in breach has two choices. He can choose to terminate a contract and claim compensation, or he can choose to continue with the contract and claim compensation. If he decides to terminate his contract, he must communicate his intention to terminate to the person who breached the contract.

The case study of South West Water below provides an example of a very serious breach of contract which causes a right of termination to arise.

Case study: South West Water Services Limited v International Computers Limited (1997)

The South West Water company made a claim for breach of contract against International Computers Limited ('ICL'). It had entered into a contract where ICL had agreed to supply a computer system to the water company. The computer system was required to be installed in time for South West Water to be able to bill water customers in 1997. It also wanted to make savings that complied with the targets set by the water regulation authority, OFWAT. The water company claimed that ICL had breached the contract by failing to deliver the computer systems.

The matter was resolved at court. The key facts are set out below:

- Completion of the system was due by the end of October 1995. From the beginning of the project ICL had problems meeting the deadline. Therefore, the companies agreed to revise the deadline for completion to October 1996.

- Further delays occurred. ICL requested another revised deadline of November 1997.

- In March 1996 at a meeting, South West Water informed ICL that it would terminate the contract as it did not believe that ICL could comply with the current deadline.

The court decided that the delay in relation to the revised deadline by ICL was a breach which was so serious that South West Water was entitled to terminate the contract and claim compensation for non-delivery of the computer system. ICL knew that installation of the computer system was required for the 1997 billing period and it was clear from the facts of the case that there was a high risk that the dates could not be complied with. ICL was aware of this when it proposed the initial completion dates when it won the contract. The court concluded that:

- the delay by ICL was so serious as to defeat the commercial purpose of the contract;

- the behaviour of ICL amounted to a refusal to perform the contract in a reasonable time;

- attempts to propose new deadlines did not affect South West Water's right to terminate the contract. This was because the behaviour of ICL had substantially deprived South West Water of all of the benefits of the contract.

South West Water was entitled to recover all of the money it had paid to ICL.

It is not always a straightforward situation when trying to assess if the other party to your contract has committed a serious breach of contract which would entitle you to terminate the contract. Therefore, you should obtain advice in relation to your specific situation to determine whether you have any right of termination or other remedies available.

Compensation

The usual remedy for breach of contract is 'damages', i.e. monetary compensation. The purpose of damages is to put the person who has not caused the breach in the position he should have been in (to the extent that is possible) if the contract had been performed. The general rules regarding damages (i.e. compensation) are discussed in chapter 4. However, it is useful to again refer to this matter here.

The general rules regarding compensation for breach of contract are that a person who has entered into a contract should be compensated for losses he has incurred due to the other person's breach of contract. These losses are those which were reasonably foreseeable at the time the contract was entered into as likely to be caused by the breach of contract. He is not entitled to be compensated for losses which were not reasonably foreseeable as being likely to be caused by the breach of contract (often referred to as 'indirect losses').

Therefore, the compensation he can receive can depend on the facts of the matter. However, compensation may include recovering money paid, loss of profits, as well as compensation for additional costs which may have been incurred as a result of the breach (e.g. paying for another supplier to correctly carry out work which has been carried out under the contract or does not conform to the contract requirements).

For example, you have agreed to supply sewing machines to a client who manufactures lingerie. He informs you that his current machines are old and unreliable and keep breaking down. He has also told you that he is very concerned that he will lose some of his clients (as he has received complaints from his existing clients) as well as not being able to take on new work. Therefore, he is replacing the old machines with your machines. You deliver the machines. However, 50 per cent of the machines are defective. It takes six weeks to replace the defective machines. As a result of these defective machines, you will now be liable for the following losses:

- The cost of replacing the defective machines.

- The loss of profits on lingerie sales that he would have usually made to customers.

- The costs incurred in using alternative companies to carry out sewing work that your client could not carry out due to the lack of working machines.

As you had been made aware of your client's situation, you would have been aware that such losses would be likely to be caused by your breach of contract (i.e. the supply of defective machines). If you have a written contract in place with your client, there may be a limit of liability or clauses excluding liability for financial losses.

Alternatively, you may find that if you are in breach of contract (e.g. you supply defective goods or fail to deliver goods), your client is entitled under the Sale of Goods Act 1979 to offset costs he has incurred in going to another supplier against money that he owes you under the contract. This was the position in the Lidl case discussed in chapter 3. In the Lidl case, the court confirmed that Lidl was entitled to offset the costs it incurred in using an alternative supplier against the money owed to Hertford for the deliveries actually made.

Legal action

If you do find yourself in the unfortunate situation of having to start or defend legal proceedings, it is important to obtain legal advice.

You need to know the strength of your claim or defence. Rather than pursuing litigation or defending a claim, you may find the most practical and cost-effective method of dealing with the situation is to negotiate a settlement. Your lawyer should be able to assist you with finding the most effective strategy for your situation.

You can start or defend legal proceedings without a lawyer. However, you may find yourself at a serious disadvantage if the other person involved in the legal proceedings is using a lawyer. Guidance can be found on the Court Service's website (www.courtservice.gov.uk) regarding starting and defending legal proceedings.

The right to sue is subject to a time period known as a 'limitation period'. You also need to know if the claim is within this period. For breach of contract claims, the general rule is six years from when the breach of contract took place.

If you are the defendant, do not just ignore papers from the court as you may find that the judgment is awarded against you if you do nothing. Even if you do obtain legal advice, you may want to familiarise yourself with the procedures involved in litigation. As referred to above, details can be obtained from the Court Service's website at www.courtservice.gov.uk.

Your contract may contain a clause requiring disputes to be resolved by methods other than litigation, such as arbitration. You should again obtain legal advice regarding the most appropriate action to take in relation to a claim you may have or a claim made against you that will be dealt with by arbitration.

Arbitration is sometimes regarded as being more cost effective and quicker than court proceedings, but this may not always be true in practice. Although lawyers are not necessary, they are usually involved as they understand the rules and procedures and have experience of dealing with disputes. Arbitration involves an independent person or persons (who may often be experts in relation to the subject matter of the dispute or the industries of the contracting parties) hearing evidence, reviewing facts and providing a decision. There are recognised arbitration bodies that have their own rules which they apply to arbitration; for example, there is the London Court of International Arbitration (www.lcia-arbitration. com). Arbitrators are often specialists in relation to the relevant business or industries.

 One of the benefits of arbitration is that it takes place in a private tribunal.

A clause in international contracts is often included requiring disputes to be resolved by arbitration. This is because neither party wants to use the national courts of the other person's country, as well as preferring the private arrangements for resolving disputes. For example, the ICC (International Chamber of Commerce) provides arbitration services which are often used in relation to international contracts. Details can be found on its website at www.iccwbo.org/index_court.asp.

Alternative dispute resolution

Mediation is an alternative method of resolving disputes and is now becoming popular. Mediation involves a neutral third party working with the parties involved in the dispute to come up with a solution or settlement. Information on mediation and other services can be found on the Centre for Effective Dispute Resolution's (CEDR) website. CEDR is a not-for-profit organisation and its website is www.cedr.co.uk.

Summary of key points

- In the event of a dispute, gather all of the relevant information.
- Notify your insurers and obtain legal advice.
- Don't make admissions without professional advice.
- Consider alternative dispute resolution if applicable.

CHAPTER 9

Getting the best out of your lawyer

What you'll find in this chapter

✔ Choosing your lawyer
✔ Working with your lawyer
✔ Complaints

When you run a business it is important to select the right management team. It is just as important to select good external professional advisers. Various professional advisers can assist you in relation to your legal affairs, such as consultants or lawyers. The expression 'lawyer' is used in this chapter to refer to solicitors and barristers. This chapter focuses on the issues you need to consider when selecting and working with your lawyer.

 A good practical lawyer can be invaluable to your business.

Choosing your lawyer

• Most people usually consider using a solicitor when they need legal advice. However, due to recent changes, members of the public, under a scheme known as Public Access, can directly use the services of barristers who have undergone Public Access training. Traditionally, members of the public could not obtain services directly from a barrister. They had to use a solicitor, who would then instruct the barrister. For example, if there was a specialist point of law upon which expert legal advice was required, a solicitor would instruct a barrister. As with solicitors, communications between barristers and their clients are protected by legal privilege. There are some differences in relation to the services offered by barristers and solicitors (e.g. a barrister cannot send a letter on your behalf on his stationery and sign it, unlike a solicitor). The Bar Council (the professional body which regulates barristers' activities) has issued guidance on Public Access and the role of barristers. The guidance can be found on the Bar Council's website at www.barcouncil.org.uk/documents/PublicAccess_GuidanceForLayClients_Aug04.pdf.

As this Public Access scheme is relatively new, it is not clear to what extent the public will want to go directly to a barrister rather than a solicitor whom they would normally use. However, there are some obvious cost benefits of being able to go directly to a barrister; for example, in relation to advice on a complex contract issue (which a solicitor may not be able to deal with and he would need to go to a barrister for assistance). The details regarding the Public Access scheme have been included so that users of this book are aware of the options that are available to them.

- Personal recommendation is one of the best methods of finding a lawyer for your business. If you are a member of a trade or professional association, it may be able to make recommendations or offer access to legal services provided at a preferential rate to their members. You could also contact local business support organisations, such as a Chamber of Commerce.

- You can also search legal directories or online databases. You can search the Law Society's online database for solicitors at www.law society.org.uk/choosingandusing/findasolicitor.law. You can also search the Bar Directory (2.sweetandmaxwell.co.uk/bardirectory/website), which can be accessed directly or through the Bar Council's website (www.barcouncil.org.uk) for details of barristers who work under the Public Access scheme.

- Select a lawyer with experience in the area in which you need help. There is no point going to a divorce lawyer if you need help with a contract selling IT equipment and services.

- Most lawyers will offer you a free consultation. These usually last between 30 minutes and one hour. You should make the most of this consultation:

  1. Go to the consultation with a list of questions and points that you would like to discuss.

  2. Use the consultation to assess the lawyer. You will want someone who understands you and your business.

  3. Lawyers are trained to understand difficult legal concepts. Accordingly, a good lawyer should be able to explain legal concepts to you in terms that you can understand. Use the consultation to assess the lawyer's ability to provide clear explanations and advice.

Assuming you are happy with the consultation and you decide to work with a particular lawyer, some further points are set out below to assist you.

Working with your lawyer

- Lawyers usually charge on an hourly basis. This means that you will be charged for all the work he carries out in relation to your matter. Sometimes clients are shocked when they receive their first bill as all activities are charged for; for example, writing emails, telephone calls, writing notes of meetings, travelling and attending meetings, etc.

- Some lawyers are now offering to carry out work on a fixed-price basis. Ask your lawyer if he is willing to.

- If you decide to select a lawyer who works on an hourly-fee basis, ask him to provide you with an estimate of the cost of your matter. Lawyers should provide this information in their terms and conditions of business (sometimes called a 'client care letter'). The lawyer's terms will usually contain a description of the work he will carry out and the details of his fees.

- You should also ask your lawyer to let you know when he is getting close to reaching the estimated cost.

Complaints

- If you are not happy with the service you have received from your lawyer, you should follow the solicitor's firm's (or the barrister's chamber's) complaints procedure.

- If your complaint is not resolved to your satisfaction, you should contact the relevant regulatory professional body, i.e. the Consumer Complaints Service (which is part of the Law Society) or Bar Council. The Law Society requires complaints about solicitors (not related to costs) to be made within six months of the work your solicitor carried out for you or within six months from the solicitor's final response to your complaint (whichever is the later).

- If the complaint relates to your bill, you can ask your solicitor to apply for a remuneration certificate in relation to non-contentious work (i.e. non-court work), which will be issued by the Consumer Complaints Service. This certificate will give an assessment regarding the fairness of the charges. You are required to make the application to your solicitor within one to three months, depending upon the circumstances. Further details can be obtained from the Law Society's website or by contacting the Consumer Complaints Service helpline on 0845 608 6565.

- The Bar Council also requires complaints to be made to it within six months of the complaint with your barrister occurring. Full details can be obtained from its website.

Glossary

The meanings of various legal terms and expressions you may come across are described in simple practical expressions below. They are not intended to be precise legal definitions. These legal terms and expressions are described using general examples of situations where relevant. These examples are not intended to cover every situation and are only provided as illustrations to assist your understanding.

Assignment	In relation to a contract, rights under a contract can be assigned (e.g. the right to receive payment can be assigned). Obligations under a contract cannot be transferred by assignment. However, the persons who have entered into a contract may often include restrictions on assignment (e.g. assignment can only take place with consent). Other examples of assignments include assignment of leases, copyright and patents.
Consideration	Consideration can be thought of as an exchange of something of value (even if it is of minimal value) for a promise, usually, payment of money in exchange for the supply of services or goods.
Contract	A contract is a legally binding agreement which creates enforceable rights and obligations. For example, you may enter into a contract with a supplier of DVDs to buy 1,000 DVDs. You and the supplier both have rights and responsibilities. The supplier is under an obligation to deliver the DVDs and has a right to be paid. The supplier delivers the DVDs and you are under an obligation to pay him.

Copyright	Copyright is an intellectual property right which protects certain works (e.g. musical, dramatic, artistic and literary work) as soon as they are created. Examples of works protected by copyright include software, books, designs, films, songs, etc. One of the main rights that a copyright owner has is the exclusive right to copy the copyrighted work.
Force Majeure	This term is used to describe an event which is outside of the control of contract parties and which affects the performance of the contract (e.g. war, acts of terrorism, floods, etc.). A clause, often included in contracts, is known as a Force Majeure clause. The purpose of this clause is to prevent liability and a breach of contract occurring as the person affected by the event may be unable to carry out his contractual obligations. The clause will usually suspend or delay the performance of the contract obligations by the person affected by the Force Majeure event, so that he is not in breach of contract. The term Force Majeure is not a defined term in English and Welsh law and should always be defined when used in a contract.
Indemnity	An indemnity is a statement confirming responsibility for paying compensation in the event that loss or damages occur or some form of wrongdoing occurs. Indemnity clauses are often found in contracts requiring the parties to indemnify the other party in certain situations; for example, 'The seller will indemnify the customer for all loss and damages incurred by the customer as a result of the seller's breach of contract'. This means that the seller will pay the customer for all his loss and damages due to the seller's breach of contract.
Intellectual property rights	Intellectual rights protect creative and inventive outputs and work. For example, a patent can protect your invention, while copyright can protect a book that you have written and your company logo may be protected by a registered trade mark. In the UK,

	some of the rights require registration at the Patent Office to protect them, while rights such as copyright (referred to above) do not require it.
Liability	Liability is a legal responsibility; for example, Mr Smith is personally liable for his company's debts because he gave a guarantee to the lender.
Patent	A patent is an intellectual property right which protects inventions. A patent application is required for the protection of this right and is filed at the Patent Office.
Trade mark	A trade mark is an intellectual property right. Trade marks can include logos, names of businesses, expressions and jingles. Trade marks can be registered. They identify the goods and services of one business from those of another. The owner of a registered trade mark has the exclusive right to use that trade mark in relation to the goods and services relating to the trade mark registration in the country or countries where that trade mark is registered.

APPENDIX 1

Checklists

As discussed in chapter 3, you may find yourself in the position of carrying out work on the basis of the standard terms and conditions of another business (e.g. your client or a key supplier/subcontractor). As previously mentioned, these terms will be drafted to provide the maximum benefit for your client or supplier/subcontractor. It is important that you understand these terms and how they affect you.

The checklists below provide some basic items which may require your specific attention. The checklists are not exhaustive or exclusive. In addition, you may have some specific requirements.

You should refer to the checklist at the back of chapter 4 to remind yourself of the points you need to consider when drawing up your own standard terms.

Checklist for client's terms

Property and risk

Have you checked the clauses to see when risk and property (i.e. ownership) pass to your client? ☐

You want to avoid situations where the responsibility for loss or damage (i.e. risk) remains with you after delivery or ownership passes to your client before you have received payment. Such clauses can be a problem (e.g. where payment has not been received by the seller before the products have been delivered). There are a number of risks associated with this type of arrangement; for example, if the client disappears with the goods or goes into liquidation while in possession of the goods. You will not get paid or you will be an unsecured creditor in relation to the liquidation and will probably receive only a small amount of the money owed to you (as you will be given a share of the liquidated company's assets, which must be distributed amongst all the creditors). You should try to negotiate a change to this clause if required (e.g. ownership passes on payment and risk passes on delivery).

Payment

In your payment terms, does your client have any right to deduct or withhold payments in the event of a dispute? ☐

You should try to negotiate an amendment to this clause to avoid the clause being exercised unreasonably.

Intellectual property rights

Have you checked the clauses dealing with the transfer of intellectual property rights (e.g. copyright) which have been created in the course of carrying out the services or work? ☐

These clauses will have to be amended if you need to use these intellectual property rights.

Warranties

Can you comply with the warranties? ☐

Are these clauses consistent with any specific requirements you have in your contract with your client? ☐

Time for performance

Is time of the essence in relation to the performance of a specific obligation? ☐

Do you have to deliver the goods by a specified date? ☐

Unless you are very confident that you can comply with time specifications, you should include a specific statement that time is not of the essence.

Liabilities

Have you contractually agreed to any clauses accepting
liabilities that are greater than such that would be imposed
under general law? ☐

Sometimes liability clauses can be very widely drafted. You should try to
avoid accepting such clauses.

Does your insurance cover your liability under the contract? ☐

If there is no limit on your liabilities in the contract, try to negotiate a
limit.

Termination

Do any of the rights of termination affect your right to receive
payment for work carried out or goods delivered before the
date of termination? ☐

Checklist for supplier's/subcontractor's terms

Changes

Does the supplier/subcontractor have an unrestricted right to
make changes to the services or products he is supplying to you? ☐

Time for performance

Have you committed to carry out work for your client within
a specified time and if so, have you made sure that your
suppliers/subcontractors have similar obligations to you? ☐

Some time-related obligations may state that 'time is not of the
essence'. If you have committed to such an obligation, you should try to
negotiate with those suppliers/subcontractors who you are dependent
on, changing your requirements in their contracts to 'time is of the
essence'.

Liabilities

Are there any limits on liability and if so, is the limit
unreasonably low? ☐

Consider your potential loss if things go wrong due to your supplier and you have to compensate your client then claim money from your supplier. It is unlikely that your supplier will agree to remove any standard limits, but you may be able to negotiate a higher limit.

Termination and suspension

What are the circumstances and time limits for exercising the rights of termination or suspension? ☐

Have a look at any rights of termination or suspension. If you are dependent on your suppliers/subcontractors for supplying your services or goods to your client, you will not be in a good position if they leave you and you cannot perform your contract.

Subcontracting

Is there an unrestricted right for a supplier/subcontractor to subcontract his obligations or work? ☐

If this right is exercised, it may affect the quality of the work or products you are supplying to your client. You should restrict this right so that it can only be exercised with your written permission.

APPENDIX 2

Example contracts

Examples of contracts for supply of goods or services are included in this section of the book. These contracts are basic examples for general illustration purposes. It is recommended that you obtain professional advice for your specific situation.

Contract for supply of services

Date: _____

Parties: _____

(1)   [*insert name of supplier*] ('Supplier') with [*a registered office/an address*] at [*insert address*]; and

(2)   [*insert name of buyer*] ('Buyer') with [*a registered office/an address*] at [*insert address*].

Introduction

This Agreement sets out the terms and conditions upon which the Supplier agrees to supply the Services described in this Agreement to the Buyer.

1.   Definitions

1.1   In this Agreement, the following words shall have the following meanings:

'Agreement' means this agreement including the attached schedule, as amended from time to time.

'Buyer' has the meaning described above.

'Services' shall mean the services described in the attached schedule.

'Price' shall be the price payable for the Services by the Buyer, as specified in the attached schedule.

'Supplier' has the meaning described above.

1.2   Headings are inserted for convenience only and shall not affect the construction of this Agreement.

2.   Services

The Supplier shall supply the Services specified in the attached

Contract for supply of services (continued)

schedule to the Buyer. Any times quoted in relation to the performance of the Services are estimates. Time shall not be of the essence in relation to the performance of the Services.

3. **Warranty**

The Supplier shall supply the Services to the Buyer with reasonable care and skill. Except as stated in the preceding sentence, all warranties or conditions in relation to the Services, whether express or implied (by statute or otherwise), shall be excluded to the fullest extent permitted by law.

4. **Intellectual property**

Copyright and all other intellectual property rights created by the Supplier in performing the Services shall belong to the Supplier. However, the Supplier grants the Buyer a licence to use such rights created by the Supplier on a non-exclusive basis to the extent necessary for the purpose of using the Services or any products or materials created by the Supplier as a result of the Services which are provided to the Buyer, subject to receiving all the sums payable by the Buyer to the Seller under this Agreement.

5. **Price and payment**

5.1 The Buyer shall pay the Price for the Services together with VAT.

5.2 The Buyer shall pay the Supplier the Price plus VAT within 14 days of the date of the Supplier's invoice, which shall be delivered upon completion of the Services. Time shall be of the essence in relation to payment.

6. **Liabilities**

6.1 Subject to Clause 6.3, the Supplier's liability for any losses, claims, damages or expenses arising out of or in connection with this Agreement, howsoever caused, including by negligence, breach of duty (statutory or otherwise), breach of contract or otherwise shall not exceed [*insert limit*].

6.2   Subject to Clause 6.3, the Supplier shall not be liable to the Buyer for any loss of profit, anticipated savings, business interruption or for any indirect or consequential loss incurred by the Buyer, howsoever caused, including by negligence, breach of duty (statutory or otherwise), breach of contract or otherwise and whether or not such losses were foreseeable at the time of entering into this Agreement.

6.3   Nothing in this Agreement shall exclude or restrict liability for the Supplier's fraud, death or personal injury due to the Supplier's negligence.

7.   Force Majeure

Neither party shall be liable for delays in performing or failure to perform any of their obligations under this Agreement due to any event outside of their reasonable control (including, without limitation, war, floods, acts of terrorism, official strike) which delays or prevents them from performing any of their obligations under this Agreement. They shall inform the other party in writing, as soon as practicably possible, when such event occurs. If this event continues to delay or prevent performance for more than [*insert figure*] days from the date of notification, either party can terminate this Agreement with immediate effect by giving written notice to the other party.

8.   Termination

8.1   Either party can terminate this Agreement:

(a)   by 14 days' written notice to the other party; or

Contract for supply of services (continued)

(b) with immediate effect by written notice to the other party if the other party is in material breach of any of its obligations under this Agreement; or

(c) with immediate effect by written notice to the other party if the other party goes into liquidation, becomes bankrupt, makes a voluntary arrangement with its creditors, or a receiver or an administrator is appointed in respect of its business; or

(d) in accordance with Clause 7.

8.2 The Buyer shall pay the Supplier for any Services performed before termination.

9. Notices

Any notices which need to be given under this Agreement shall be sent in writing to either party's registered office address or principal place of business, unless otherwise notified.

10. Assignment

Neither party can assign its rights under this Agreement without the consent of the other party, which shall not be unreasonably withheld.

11. Waiver

No failure by either party to exercise any of its rights under this Agreement shall be deemed to be a waiver of such rights or prevent the exercise of such rights at a later date.

12. Third-party rights

No-one who is not a party to this Agreement has any benefit or any right to enforce any term of this Agreement for the purposes of the Contracts (Rights of Third Parties) Act 1999.

Contract for supply of services (continued)

13. Applicable law and dispute resolution

This Agreement, and any disputes which may arise in connection with it, shall be governed by and construed in accordance with English and Welsh law and the parties shall submit to the exclusive jurisdiction of the English and Welsh courts.

14. Entire agreement

14.1 This Agreement constitutes the entire agreement and understanding of the parties and supersedes any previous agreement and understanding between the parties relating to the supply of the Services by the Supplier to the Buyer.

14.2 The Buyer acknowledges and agrees that in entering into this Agreement, it does not rely on any statement, representation or warranty of the Supplier (other than which are expressly set out in this Agreement). Nothing in this clause shall operate to limit or exclude any liability for fraud.

14.3 Variations to this Agreement can only be made in writing by the agreement of the parties and signed by their authorised representatives.

This Agreement is made between the parties on the date shown on the first page of this Agreement.

Signed upon behalf of [*insert name of Supplier*] by:

Signature: _____

Name: _____

Position: _____

Contract for supply of services (continued)

Signed upon behalf of [*insert name of Buyer*] by:

Signature: _____

Name: _____

Position: _____

Contract for supply of services (continued)

SCHEDULE

Services: [*insert description/scope of services*]

Price: [*insert price*]

Contract for sale of goods

Date: _____

Parties: _____

(1)   [*insert name of supplier*] ('Seller') with [*a registered office/an address*] at [*insert address*]; and

(2)   [*insert name of buyer*] ('Buyer') with [*a registered office/an address*] at [*insert address*].

Introduction

This Agreement sets out the terms and conditions upon which the Seller agrees to sell the goods described in this Agreement to the Buyer.

1.   Definitions

1.1   In this Agreement, the following words shall have the following meanings:

'Agreement' means this agreement including the attached schedule, as amended from time to time.

'Buyer' has the meaning described above.

'Goods' shall mean the goods, items or products described in the attached schedule.

'Price' shall be the price payable for the Goods by the Buyer, as specified in the attached schedule.

'Seller' has the meaning described above.

1.2   Headings are inserted for convenience only and shall not affect the construction of this Agreement.

2.   Goods

The Seller shall supply the Goods specified in the attached schedule to the Buyer. The Goods shall be delivered after the Seller

Contract for sale of goods (continued)

has notified the Buyer that the Goods are ready for despatch. Any times given for delivery are estimates only. Time shall not be of the essence in relation to the delivery of the Goods.

3.   Risk and title

3.1   Risk of loss or of damage to the Goods shall pass from the Seller to the Buyer on delivery of the Goods to the Buyer's premises or another place agreed between the parties.

3.2   The title shall not pass to the Buyer until full payment of the Price in cleared funds is received by the Seller.

4.   Warranty

The Seller warrants the Goods supplied under this Agreement shall comply with any specification contained in the attached schedule and are free from defects in workmanship and materials for 12 months from the date of delivery. Except as stated in the preceding sentence, all warranties or conditions in relation to the Goods, whether express or implied (by statute or otherwise), shall be excluded to the fullest extent permitted by law.

5.   Price and payment

5.1   The Buyer shall pay the Price for the Goods together with any delivery charges specified in the attached schedule. The Buyer shall also pay VAT in addition to the Price and delivery charges.

5.2   The Buyer shall pay the Seller the Price and any other charges due within 14 days of the date of the Seller's invoice, which shall be delivered on the date of the delivery of the Goods. Time is of the essence in relation to payment.

6.   Liabilities

6.1   Subject to Clause 6.3, the Seller's liability for any losses, claims,

Contract for sale of goods (continued)

damages or expenses arising out of or in connection with this Agreement, howsoever caused, including by negligence, breach of duty (statutory or otherwise), breach of contract or otherwise shall not exceed [*insert limit*].

6.2 Subject to Clause 6.3, the Seller shall not be liable to the Buyer for any loss of profit, anticipated savings, business interruption or for any indirect or consequential loss incurred by the Buyer, howsoever caused, including by negligence, breach of duty (statutory or otherwise), breach of contract or otherwise and whether or not such losses were foreseeable at the time of entering into this Agreement.

6.3 Nothing in this Agreement shall exclude or restrict liability for:

(a) the Seller's fraud; or

(b) death or personal injury due to the Seller's negligence; or

(c) the breach of any of the Seller's obligations arising from Section 12 of the Sale of Goods Act 1979 which cannot be legally excluded.

7. Force Majeure

Neither party shall be liable for delays in performing or failure to perform any of their obligations under this Agreement due to any event outside of their reasonable control (including, without limitation, war, floods, terrorism, official strikes) which delays or prevents them from performing any of their obligations under this Agreement. They shall inform the other party in writing, as soon as practicably possible, when such an event occurs. If this event continues to delay or prevent performance for more than [*insert figure*] days from the date of notification, either party can terminate this Agreement with immediate effect by giving written notice to the other party.

Contract for sale of goods (continued)

8. Termination

8.1 Either party can terminate this Agreement:

(a) by 14 days' written notice to the other party; or

(b) with immediate effect by written notice to the other party if the other party is in material breach of any of its obligations under this Agreement; or

(c) with immediate effect by written notice to the other party if the other party goes into liquidation, becomes bankrupt, makes a voluntary arrangement with its creditors, or a receiver or an administrator is appointed in respect of its business; or

(d) in accordance with Clause 7.

8.2 The Buyer shall pay the Seller for any Goods delivered or for any costs incurred in carrying out its obligations before termination.

9. Notices

Any notices which need to be given under this Agreement shall be sent in writing to either party's registered office address or principal place of business, unless otherwise notified.

10. Assignment

Neither party can assign its rights under this Agreement without the consent of the other party, which shall not be unreasonably withheld.

11. Waiver

No failure by either party to exercise any of its rights under this Agreement shall be deemed to be a waiver of such rights or prevent the exercise of such rights at a later date.

Contract for sale of goods (continued)

12. Third-party rights

No-one who is not a party to this Agreement has any benefit or any right to enforce any term of this Agreement for the purposes of the Contracts (Rights of Third Parties) Act 1999.

13. Applicable law and dispute resolution

This Agreement, and any disputes which may arise in connection with it, shall be governed by and construed in accordance with English and Welsh law and the parties shall submit to the exclusive jurisdiction of the English and Welsh courts.

14. Entire agreement

14.1 This Agreement constitutes the entire agreement and understanding of the parties and supersedes any previous agreement and understanding between the parties relating to the sale of the Goods by the Seller to the Buyer.

14.2 The Buyer acknowledges and agrees that in entering into this Agreement, it does not rely on any statement, representation or warranty of the Seller (other than which are expressly set out in this Agreement). Nothing in this clause shall operate to limit or exclude any liability for fraud.

14.3 Variations to this Agreement can only be made in writing by the agreement of the parties and signed by their authorised representatives.

This Agreement is made between the parties on the date shown on the first page of this Agreement.

Signed upon behalf of [*insert name of Seller*] by:

Contract for sale of goods (continued)

Signature: _____

Name: _____

Position: _____

Signed upon behalf of [*insert name of Buyer*] by:

Signature: _____

Name: _____

Position: _____

Contract for sale of goods (continued)

SCHEDULE

Goods: [*insert description*]

Price: [*insert price*]

Delivery charges: [*insert delivery charges if applicable*]

Specification: [*include any specification as referred to in Clause 4 if relevant*]

APPENDIX 3

Useful contacts

Bar Council

The Bar Council is the professional body which regulates the activities of barristers.

289–293 High Holborn   Tel: 020 7242 0082
London WC1V 7HZ   Website: www.barcouncil.org.uk

Centre for Effective Dispute Resolution

The Centre for Effective Dispute Resolution provides mediation and other alternative dispute resolution services.

International Dispute   Tel: 020 7536 6000
Resolution Centre   Website: www.cedr.co.uk
70 Fleet Street
London EC4Y 1EU

Companies House

Companies House provides details on setting up a company and related information and guidance. Reports and details can be obtained about companies.

Companies House   Tel: 0870 333 3636
Crown Way   Website: www.companieshouse.
Maindy   gov.uk
Cardiff CF14 3UZ

Court Service

The Court Service has the responsibility for running most courts in England and Wales. The Court Service's website contains useful information regarding court procedures.

Customer Service Unit
5th Floor, Clive House
Petty France
London SW1H 9HD

Tel: 020 7189 2000 or 0845 568 770
Website: www.courtservice.gov.uk

Export Credits Guarantee Department

The Export Credits Guarantee Department (ECGD) is a government department which provides a range of financial products to UK exporters.

London office:
PO Box 2200
2 Exchange Tower
Harbour Exchange Square
London E14 9GS

Tel: 020 7512 7000
Website: www.ecgd.gov.uk

Cardiff office:
Lambourne House
Lambourne Crescent
Llanishen
Cardiff CF14 5GL

Tel: 029 2032 8500
Website: www.ecgd.gov.uk

ICC International Court of Arbitration

The ICC International Court of Arbitration provides arbitration services.

General enquiries:
Emmanuel Jolivet
General Counsel

Tel: (00 33) 1 4953 2943
Email: webmaster_court@iccwbo.org

United Kingdom:
John Merrett
Arbitration Consultant

Tel: 020 7792 8579
Email: johnmerrett@iccorg.co.uk

30 Chepstow Road
London W2 5BE

Website: www.iccwbo.org/home/
menu_international_arbitration.
asp

Information Commissioner

The Information Commissioner has responsibility for data protection matters. The Information Commissioner's website provides information and guidance on data protection, privacy and public access to official information.

Wycliffe House
Water Lane
Wilmslow
Cheshire SK9 5AF

Tel: 01625 545 745
Website: www.information
commissioner.gov.uk

Insolvency Service

Information about insolvency procedures can be found on the Insolvency Service's website. Bankruptcy searches can also be carried out on its website.

21 Bloomsbury Street
London WC1B 3QW

Tel: 020 7291 6895
Website: www.insolvency.gov.uk

International Chamber of Commerce

The International Chamber of Commerce provides information and guidance in relation to international business matters. Details of Incoterms can also be found on its website.

38 Cours Albert 1er
75008 Paris
France

Tel: (00 33) 1 4953 2828
Website: www.iccwbo.org

Law Society

The Law Society is the professional body which regulates solicitors' activities. Its website contains an online database of solicitors.

113 Chancery Lane
London WC2A 1PL

Tel: 020 7242 1222

London Court of International Arbitration

The Court of Arbitration provides arbitration as well as other dispute resolution services.

70 Fleet Street
London EC4Y 1EU

Tel: 020 7936 7007
Website: www.lcia-arbitration.com

Office for Harmonization in the Internal Market (Trade Marks and Design)

The Office for Harmonization in the Internal Market (Trade Marks and Design) registers Community Trade Marks and Register Community Designs. Useful information and guidance can be found on its website.

Avenida de Europa, 4
E-03008 Alicante
Spain

Tel: (00 34) 9 6513 9100
Website: oami.eu.int

Patent Office

The Patent Office is responsible for intellectual property in the UK. Its website contains useful information and guidance on intellectual property as well as registration forms.

Concept House
Cardiff Road
Newport
South Wales NP10 8QQ

Tel: 0845 950 0505
Website: www.patent.gov.uk

Registry Trust

Details of County court judgments can be found on the Registry Trust's website.

173–175 Cleveland Street
London W1T 6QR

Tel: 020 7380 0133
Website: www.registry-trust.org.uk

UK Trade & Investment

UK Trade & Investment is a government organisation which provides support and assistance to UK businesses that want to develop their business overseas.

Website: www.uktradeinvest.gov.uk

Index

C

K
knowledge

MORE BOOKS AVAILABLE FROM LAWPACK

Employment Law Made Easy

Written by an employment law solicitor, *Employment Law Made Easy* is a comprehensive, reader-friendly source of information that will provide answers to practically all your employment law questions. Essential knowledge for employers and employees. Valid for use in England & Wales, and Scotland.

Code B702 | ISBN 1 904053 88 2 | Paperback | 153 x 234mm | 224pp | £11.99 | 6th edition

Health & Safety at Work Essentials

Every workplace has to comply with an extensive range of health and safety rules and regulations. With more legal claims being made daily, the price for failing to comply, whether through fines or claims by employees, can be high. This handy, 'one-stop' handbook sets out the background legal basics and provides succinct, practical advice on what measures to take.

Code B435 | ISBN 1 904053 77 7 | Paperback | 153 x 234mm | 176pp | £9.99 | 4th edition

Leaves on the Line!

Faulty goods, shoddy service, poor advice... these are things most of us, at some time, feel we have good reason to complain about. In this handbook, Steve Wiseman draws on his extensive experience as a Citizens Advice Bureau manager and tells you how to ensure your complaint has maximum impact, whether it be against your local shop or a government department.

Code B430 | ISBN 1 904053 67 X | Paperback | A5 | 208pp | £7.99 | 2nd edition

To order, visit **www.lawpack.co.uk** or call **020 7394 4040**

MORE BOOKS AVAILABLE FROM **LAWPACK**

Residential Lettings

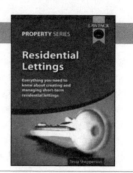

Are you thinking of letting a flat or a house? This guide steers anyone who intends – or already is – letting property through the legal and practical issues involved. It provides all the up-to-date information and tips that a would-be landlord needs. It will also alert existing landlords to the points of good practice that make a letting successful, and the legal obligations that they may not be aware of.

Code B622 | ISBN 1 904053 90 4 | Paperback | 153 x 234mm | 160pp | £11.99 | 5th edition

The Buy-to-Let Bible

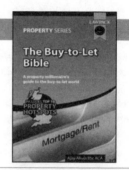

Low mortgage rates and under-performance by traditional savings and investment products means that property has never looked a better way to invest for the future. Author Ajay Ahuja divulges the practical and financial techniques that have made him a millionaire. It covers finding the right property, the right mortgage lender, the right tenant, legal issues and tax.

Code B637 | ISBN 1 904053 91 2 | Paperback | 153 x 234mm | 256pp | £11.99 | 3rd edition

The Seven Pillars of Buy-to-Let Wisdom

In his first, bestselling buy-to-let book, *The Buy-to-Let Bible* author and buy-to-let millionaire Ajay Ahuja provided the basics of successful buy-to-let. Ajay has now written 'further reading' for the buy-to-let investor, *The Seven Pillars of Buy-to-let Wisdom*, that explains in depth how to get the most from your investment by examining the seven fundamentals of successful buy-to-let property management.

Code B447 | ISBN 1 904053 42 4 | Paperback | 153 x 234mm | 144pp | £9.99 | 1st edition

To order, visit **www.lawpack.co.uk** or call **020 7394 4040**

MORE BOOKS AVAILABLE FROM LAWPACK

301 Legal Forms, Letters & Agreements

Our best-selling form book is now in its eighth edition. It is packed with forms, letters and agreements for legal protection in many situations. It provides a complete do-it-yourself library of 301 ready-to-use legal documents, for business or personal use. Areas covered include loans and borrowing, buying and selling, employment, transfers and assignments and residential tenancy.

Code B402 | ISBN 1 904053 66 1 | Paperback | A4 | 384pp | £19.99 | 8th edition

Personnel Manager

A book of more than 200 do-it-yourself forms, contracts and letters to help your business manage its personnel records. Areas covered include recruitment and hiring, employment contracts and agreements, handling new employees, personnel management, performance evaluation and termination of employment.

Code B417 | ISBN 1 904053 23 8 | Paperback | A4 | 268pp | £14.99 | 3rd edition

Ready-Made Company Minutes & Resolutions

Maintaining good, up-to-date records of company meetings and resolutions is not only good practice but also a legal requirement, whatever size your company is. This book of forms makes compiling minutes of board and shareholder meetings straightforward. It includes more than 125 commonly-required resolutions and minutes to save you time and effort.

Code B616 | ISBN 1 904053 73 4 | Paperback | A4 | 192pp | £14.99 | 3rd edition

To order, visit **www.lawpack.co.uk** or call **020 7394 4040**

MORE BOOKS AVAILABLE FROM LAWPACK

101 Ways to Pay Less Tax

This book provides a wealth of tax saving tips from H M Williams Chartered Accountants, a national award winning firm of chartered accountants.

The tips included in this book are all legitimate ways to help reduce your tax bill – tax avoidance rather than tax evasion.

Code B448 I ISBN 1 904053 71 8 I Paperback I 153 x 234mm I 184pp I £9.99 I 1ˢᵗ edition

Proper Coffee

Management tomes abound but they can be turgid to wade through. This book provides a refreshing alternative for the small business. It provides succinct, practical advice on how to raise the bottom line and increase profitability, without working any harder.

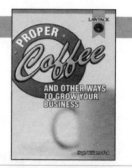

Code B451 I ISBN 1 904053 86 6 I Paperback I 153 x 234mm I 150pp I £9.99 I 1ˢᵗ edition

Tax Answers at a Glance 2005/06

We all need to get to grips with the array of taxes now levied by the government. Compiled by award-winning tax experts and presented in question-and-answer format, this handbook provides a useful and digestible summary of Income Tax, Capital Gains Tax, Inheritance Tax, pensions, self-employment, partnerships, Corporation Tax, Stamp Duty/Land Tax, VAT, and more.

Code B625 I ISBN 1 904053 76 9 I Paperback I 153 x 234mm I 208pp I £9.99 I 5ᵗʰ edition

To order, visit **www.lawpack.co.uk** or call **020 7394 4040**

Visit the new Lawpack website and order online at www.lawpack.co.uk

What's new?

We've tried to retain the ease of use of our old site, while offering much more in terms of free legal information, more comprehensive product descriptions to give a true idea of what you're buying and links to qualified solicitors and legal resources if our products aren't appropriate for your situation.

Comprehensive product listings

First and foremost, Lawpack is a DIY legal publisher, and our ever-expanding range of easy-to-use titles is brought to life on the new website with extensive product overviews, author biographies, full content details and recommendations of other complementary titles in our range.